PICTURE DICTIONARY

PICTURE DICTIONARY

KRISTEN ELIASON

Flaming Giblet Press
an imprint of Sundress Publications

Cover Design: Emily Fickenwirth

Book Design: Kristen Eliason and Emily Fickenwirth

Katakana and Kanji: Akira Kusaka

Series Editor: T.A. Noonan

Copy Editor: Marika Von Zellen

Colophon: The primary font in this book is Georgia, with additional elements in Kabel BK BT Book, Perpetua, and Helvetica. The "fG" Flaming Giblet Press logo is a combination of Lavanderia and Bebas Neue fonts.

Flaming Giblet Press is an imprint of Sundress Publications specializing in prose, cross-genre, experimental, and/or otherwise unclassifiable texts.

http://www.sundresspublications.com/fgp

for Sadako "Meme" Takuma, the hero

and for my family, who believed

in memory of Trent C. Johnson

"I begin to sing the alphabet.
It sounds like disarticulated prayer."

Kimberly Johnson
A Metaphorical God

KATAKANA, *n.*

1. A phonetic Japanese syllabary used for writing foreign words or documents. Also called "kana." **See hiragana.** [Japanese: *kata,* one, one-sided + KANA.]

-   The American Heritage Dictionary of the
    English Language, New College Edition, 1975

ア	イ	ウ	エ	オ
A	I	U	E	O
カ	キ	ク	ケ	コ
Ka	Ki	Ku	Ke	Ko
サ	シ	ス	セ	ソ
Sa	Shi	Su	Se	So
タ	チ	ツ	テ	ト
Ta	Ti	Tsu	Te	To
ナ	ニ	ヌ	ネ	ノ
Na	Ni	Nu	Ne	No
ハ	ヒ	フ	ヘ	ホ
Ha	Hi	Hu(Fu)	He	Ho
マ	ミ	ム	メ	モ
Ma	Mi	Mu	Me	Mo
ヤ		ユ		ヨ
Ya		Yu		Yo
ラ	リ	ル	レ	ロ
Ra	Ri	Ru	Re	Ro
ワ		ヲ		ン
Wa		Wo		NN

力

KA, *parti.*

Fig. 2: an orange lost in a grocery store.

1. Do, did, is, was, are, etc...? catchall questions of nationality, gender, and produce. *Oishii desu ka?* Does it taste good?
2. Or; *Are ka kore ka.* This or that.
   See also: seedless varieties.

KA, *n.*

Fig. 3: cubicles filled with children's toys and machinery.

An office.

1. Welcome to the educational department: rooms full of too-small chairs and backaches. Felt fruit for pelting children. Masterfully. One large wall-side map that holds all Disney Worlds as equals among ones' fates.

   1732 *Prologue: Elias McArthur's Gen. Hist. Asia I* ...the antechamber of the *ka* had been filled entirely with drawers; **1812** J.W. Wentsyon, tr. *An Abbreviated Exploration of the Oriental Cultures* 177 uniformed children undergoing private tutelage are met outside the last gate of the "ka," for their safety. **1957** J.G.B. Wetzel *Guide to Etiquette Abroad* 31.2 Consequently...new employees are expected to bring gifts upon first entering the ka that will become his or her primary workplace. To neglect this duty is to deny oneself an opportunity to fall in love, and will eventually drive one to produce.

   See also: handshakes across varieties of telephonic devices including: a small cellular phone with silver buttons; a large cellular phone with a flexible blue plastic covering and at least one purple stone bauble hanging from it on weekdays while the Saturday night Do Co Mo Mushroom is black-tie optional; a standard receiver connected to an early-nineties vintage beige answering machine complete with standard pink and blue plastic buttons for listening and deleting; an office phone with speed dial; a separate rotary phone for long distance calls.

-KA DO KA, *pron., a., conj., (n.)*

Fig. 4: a very small bedroom on the south side of the house, one window, glass pulls for the closet, a painted light fixture, frames and roman shutters slide in and out of view.

1. For instance, there could be too many pictures of him in this room. Too many for comfortable company-keeping. As a result, no one will come in to sit on the bed and talk in the dark. The key exception, of course.
2. [*With or without*] the late-night taco run. *Regional Dialect.*
3. On the other hand, it could be a sign that the school waited 7 months to return her phone calls. She leans quietly with her eyes shut, presently iku-[ka do ka] kimerarenai, asking for answers. It is all she knows of question-making in the slatted dark of the tiny room. *See also: 19th-Century Binary Decision Ballots*
4. *Whether or not* the tickets will be purchased.
5. Optional relocation: Japan.

1842 Young and Clark *Manifest Shepherdry* 47 His queries had left her small choice whether or not to go. Diary entries from this period include handfuls of script reading 'wakata' and 'wakata ni.' **1920** Fitzwilliam *Rouged Knees Overseas* 1.22 Take into account these four simple guidelines for...glamour in Shanghai or Kyoto: 1. Torn or clumsily-darned stockings simply will not do in locales where shoes are [optional] or removed at the door; 2. Sake should be and can be enjoyed either warmed or chilled. Temperature is gauged by [*whether or not*] you are going out or staying in. 3. Be certain to pack light perfume, wax, chocolates and, if you possibly can, a camera. 4. Light silk kimonos are essential house wear in the summer.

6. Most often, she wants to be sure that she's making the right decision. Alternately, she wants to have everything that was promised in

February, before they bought a blender together. It's important that no one take into consideration anything she was promised in February. The photographs on the wall comprise most of what remains.

KAIBO, *n.*

Fig. 5: a bright comparison of lungs.

1. (Primarily) anatomy: the bodies she has compiled between sheaves of paper are primarily:
    a. she
    b. he
   and the organs of specific days of the week, for example Monday, as it holds her attention.

   1999 H.T. Rods *Auto Body Repairs* (trans.) "We'll have it done by Monday."

2. Autopsy.
   See also: ephemeral investigations.
   See also: rib expansion.
   See also: when the hell did he actually go?

KAKEHANARERU, *vb.*

Fig. 6: a photo album. The binding has torn along the kissing picture hidden from everyone except a snatchy-handed girl after class.

1. A series of red suitcases stacked like Russian dolls against the sliding door of the airport. The largest is scuffed in a perfect line along the back.
2. A phone call composed almost entirely of, "mm mm mm. mm mm mm," etc. These take place in Idaho, Utah, California, Osaka, Kanonji, and other locations to be determined by travel and availability.
3. The distance between her voice and the coils under the plastic cap of the phone's mouthpiece measured in millimeters squared.
4. The length of a wall map measured in cubits and hops.
5. Reportage, the scheme thereof.

2005 *The Protagonist; fr. 8* at the end of this (pilgrimage) I hope to find you waiting for me on this gray island / only I am away from you. (I will return.) I sit with one seat empty so the air can hold my hand. sad trade wind.

KI, *n.*

Fig. 7: the nearest mountain rounded over with deciduous trees; or an abstraction of a mountain rounded over with deciduous trees.

1. Spirit; Soul
2. Feeling
3. Intention; inclination, specifically, the desire to speak.
   See also: blood type as personality profile. A-Gata.

KIBO, *n.*

Fig. 8.1: the form of a dove descending over the concrete ravine.

Fig. 8.2: maps the locations of internal recognition as follows: a. the gray of a housed winter. You must house at least one cold season per session; b. the white fire of at least two opened trees; corollary: ume, ume-boshi, with or without rice; c. a bath in every prefecture, located primarily by steam; d. obon, the festival of the dead.

1. A laundered intention: clean wish, white lie.
2. A greeting in formal situations, often accompanied by large boxes of chocolate for everyone in the local language factory.

   1973 Shinohara, Eika *Greetings and Expressions of Goodwill* Oh! You are like Japanese! You are like Japanese! Arigato!

3. One domestic round-trip ticket to Okinawa under the circumstances of Fig. 23 b. under the auspices of c. She takes an extra day and lies about it. Ref.

   2003 Goda Miyuki, *An Operator's Manual* 44 I am so ANGRY!!! JUST KIDDING! HAHA!

a. *She apologizes* later, faithlessly, and under no circumstances will she be fired in the rainy season. If she can touch the barbed wire of the gunji kichi and run back, she's safe.

4. Exhaustion.
   a. The finish comes early this year.
   b. Hanami brings fish in the spring.

KINJI, *n.*

Fig. 9: a hospital behind an armored gate. a street. American amusements across include 1. Down: root beer float with ice 2. Across: Kuwae Beach 3. Across: Fun-Time Ferris Wheel 2. Down: shopping.

1. (primarily) gunji kinji, *trans.* military base. The day trip there is facilitated by a map and a helpful woman at the tourist information counter, who helps her look up the word "Kuwae" to discover that it is across the street from a shopping area, beach and amusement center. The bus is full of green plaid seats, and nearly empty aside from the driver and a sleeping obachan. As long as the ocean stays to the left. Overfolding the second map of the day, she circles her stop and gestures timidly to the bus driver, "help me get here, please; if I fall asleep; show me where to get off the bus."
2. Birthland without jungle scene;
3. The impossibility of folding enough paper cranes before the breastbone collapses. The half-life of halved paper.
4. Oceanside complex or skybound memorial benches. The most prominent of these bears the inscription, "I hear your birth come late and washed, blooded and pressed to breathe, again, please again."
5. The hospital across watches the water coming like dreams on repeat. *See also: island-bound birds*

KI GA TSUKU, *vb.*

Fig. 10: physiological ramifications as diagrammed. 1. dehydration; 2. rapid hair loss; 3. twitch of the lower eye lid; 4. extensive viewing of VH1 daytime programming.

1. become aware of; notice, esp. oneself.

1933 G. Mirin *Guiding Sense and Sanity* xx. 323 what we categorize as 'knowledge' becomes structurally circular and self-reflexive, and so depends on ki ga tsuku for the conscious definition of terms. **1959** *Fathers of Criticism* VII. 47.1 When her eating habits change he immediately launches into superficial argument without cross-examination. A pivotal battle cites childhood through adolescence as individualizing time and is submitted as an evidentiary claim of ability to change without regard to the actions of the deceased [or living] predecessors. **1977** *Icarus Quarterly* Fall 105 The first illustration of the complex self-reflexive process cites ki ga tsuku as a major factor, post-meltdown. The recognition of materials and self within the fall is described at length... **1982** *Flights of Fancy and Purposefulness 16-23* Oct. 17/5 Everyone is aware of self-reflection at this point.

KINPATSU, *n.*

Fig. 11: gaijin.

1. blond hair;
2. traffic, as it is inadvertently directed by a woman with blond hair.
3. Rel. to the gaikokujin, or the familiar, gaijin, as it applies to foreign nationals working and traveling specifically in Japan.

KIKOBUN, *n.*

Fig. 12: white-clothed henro, walking sticks with bells.

1. written description of a journey

7

KU, *n.*

Fig. 13: a book filled to the top.

1. here the sea is calm
2. laying flat against the earth (*v.*)
3. stretched parachute silk

(*phrase*) **1898** G.W. Ashair *Hist. Jap. Lit.* iv. 798 The 1500s brought about the invention of a poem consisting entirely of 17 characters, or in translation, syllables. **1900** D.L. Jonesson *Soc. Japan* XVII. V. xii, The Ku, referenced as Haiku must be concise, and compact. **1902** H. Michaels *The Literature of a Nation* XXX. II. 256 The artists of Japan labor over their tiny compositions...known as either *Hokku, Haiku* and/or *Haikai*. The verse is dedicated to the caesura and must incorporate at least one epiphany. **1914** *Western Gaz.* 1 Apr. 10/1 ...haiku, comprised of three lines, each having a specific syllable count...the first being 5, the second being 7 and the third being 5. This unrhymed pattern of compression is primarily based in images and often (but not always) a clever twist. **1957** C. BROOKE-ROSE *Lang. Love* 47 Her translations of *haiku* were elegant. **1969** *Poets and the Times* 16 May 2/1 ...comprising a set of 17 sonnets, 4 sestinas and 6 haiku.

KE, *n.*

Fig. 14: a desert full of scrub grass and tumbleweed. Your Father, Who Art On Top of the Dam.

1. The parents and siblings are in a separate city and not at the airport at the beginning of the dictionary. Primary obligations are to weddings that may or may not fail.
   (Death doth not fail thee.)
2. A secondary family equals a conglomeration of four brothers, two married, their children, and three sisters, one married, her child; births = 4, adoptees = 5, children = 6, language events < 2
   a. Comparison between oranges and seedless oranges
      i. Married and pregnant or not
      ii. Wedded or not
   b. Future comparison between children and oranges
      i. Varieties include: blond
      ii. Namesakes = 1
   c. Lengthy Introductions to friends of the family
      i. Several ∞

KECHAPPU, *n.*

Fig. 15: condiments, McDonald's dipping sauces.

1. Ketchup
2. In the city, missionaries who crush over lunch will get you as much ketchup from the counter as you need. This is the only time you're brave enough to have ketchup with your fries. This is the only time that you're sure that the word for ketchup is *kechappu*.

KEKI, n.

Fig. 16: a yellow bakery near "Town Hall" where you will have to act out "Paying your taxes" and "Filing for a Gaikokujin Card."

1. Roll cakes from Meme come from the beautiful yellow French bakery across the street.
2. There is a fruit cake on camera. You buy it for the carefully glazed fruit cut into flowers. Underneath it is yellow with whipped cream. She drops the cake at least once and the fruit unfurls.
3. *Hurry up the cakes*, a clothing line of fashionable women's-wear at the Marunaka. Varieties include: "20-gauge serious answer" and "Verily, we became the cake."

KESHO, n.

Fig. 17: a screen zoomed in on a makes-mouths-happy set of lips, carefully polished and glossed. The lips are speaking English very carefully.

1. Makeup.
2. An allergic reaction to something on the eyelid, either purple or swollen, powder or pencil.
3. PENglish, registered trademark, becomes the latest project Miyuki has you dancing around. PENglish, registered trademark, is an electric pen that students use for learning English. PENglish, registered trademark, is a pen that you touch to a picture in the PENglish, registered trademark, book. When you touch the PENglish, registered trademark, pen to the PENglish, registered trademark, picture book, a PENglish, registered trademark, mouth will appear on the screen and very slowly say, " __ ."
Every day your new job is to go to the old house with your upper lip waxed so that she can film close-ups of your mouth pronouncing en-g-lish s-y-lla-bl-es, she says every sound is a syllable and right now you are paid to wear a purple dress and not to disagree. Genki, desu-ka?
See also: an infinite number of trips to the neon-sign (read: hospital) across the street. Next door, Mini Stop, the other direction, a ho-te-ru (hotel).

ヿ

- KO, *adv.*

Fig. 18: a summer kimono, yukata.

1. This way; like this; so much like this
2. Everything happened in this manner:
    first, a star streaking its tired, old body across the map of your
    hand;
    second, a synchronized ballet of crane excavators;
    third and climax, a grassless plot;
    denouement becomes rice.

KO-, *n.*

Fig. 19: red rock and waterfall.

1. Late; deceased; dead-as-a-doornail; passed on; passed away; on the
    other side; looking down on us; in our hearts; got his wings; is no
    longer with us; is always with us; gone on to a better place; gone to
    live with God; taking a dirt nap; kicked the bucket; gave up the
    ghost; bought a pine condo; croaked; gone into that good night;
    sleeping the big sleep; gone to feed the fishes; breathed his last;
    cashed in his chips; bought the farm; gone to the city of angels;
    shuffled off this mortal coil; dearly departed; checked out; mortified;
    watching over us wherever we go; gone to live with his beagle, Bagel;
    gone to the raven's haven; filling the graveyard shift; crossed over;
    wandering the elysian fields; gone the way of the earth; he's gone; we
    think he's gone;
    ex. *ko-kesuke, the late Mr. Kesuke*
2. Where the hell is he?
    We look for days, and by we, I (do not) mean you. You (she) sit(s) in
    the basement looking through her old books for him, peeling old
    pictures of him out of non-acid-free-non-archival-photo-albums,
    searching every internet search engine for him, for something she
    wanted to know, some proof. Some people searched in the reservoir.

Others started downstream and worked back to the base of the waterfall. Some people aided the Utah Fish Preservation Project. And then like blood rising to the surface of an oxygenated pool, the divers found him quietly ascending in the water.

KOKYU, *n.*

Fig. 20: ojai breathing. ouija breathing.

1. Breathing; Respiration;
   stop.

   See also: two inches of sugar water wafting toward your downslanted nose
   See also: swimming pool notices
   See also: scare tactics

KONO MAMA NI SURU, *vb.*

Fig. 21: brother, singular, one who tries in desperation to talk you out of opening the coffin, but what does he know.

1. Leave (something) as it is.

花見

HANAMI, *n.*

Fig. 1: cherry blossoms cascading toward the base of the falls.

1. this branch with its delicate snow, its ephemeral spirits, comes with
    the flood season and takes with it, when it falls, the thing you desired
    most.

サ

SA, *n.*

Fig. 22: neon street-side cross on the church, a sign, a sign.

1. Difference; gap
2. *Nichibei no sa.* Difference between Japan and the U.S.
3. The girl at the raundory counter writes durai kureaningu (*dry cleaning*), 10:00 AM, ¥950. And this is how she knows when to come back, how much to pay.
4. Knives out. In tinny headphones Thom whines to your ear
   I want you to know
   he's not coming back
5. Like he's the god of anything well he's not.

SABISHII, *adj.*

Fig. 23: road 50 before the pond.

1863 Kingstones *Land Waters* vi. 227 They drive at least once where he or she comments on the water. Variably. Commenting on the lonely, and why isn't it stagnant, this place must be so very full. **1882** *Revisiting Roads to Oku*, Gen. Elijah North 64, Marugame, lonely looking, edged in water, edged in shrubs, etched in the door on every side, one character. **1904** W. Mer 2001, the thick, wet air presses from Kanonji, the wooden temple. Below: the inland sea trading noise for abandonment and bared arms. (Timidly) Do you speak any Japanese? Are you from America? Do you like a ride home?

1. Desolations heaped upon the shore.

SABISHIGARU, vb.

Fig. 24: a swollen eyelid.

1956 C. Christian *Att.* I. iii. 59 The waiting room of the hospital is empty except for a circular couch with a central cone forming the back. *Meme, your birthdays are the same...* [you] whiten. *I know,* she says, *I know.* **1958** M. Cabellos *Man Overboard* ii. 31 Eyes flicker compulsively toward her ticket, flight number, time, and three stunning and Englishless flight attendants calling boarding groups, ni, san, shi. They don't ask for ID before taking half her ticket and her baggage claim stickers and showing her onto the extended walkway. The flight is short and rainy, and though she hopes to snorkel, she hopes she will somehow be unable to. It rains harder, but the tourist information attendant arranges the snorkeling, and gives her Okinawan bus numbers to Camp Kuwae, near American Shopping, and the beach she's seen in his baby pictures. In the morning she receives a verypolite phone call the snorkeling is cancelled. **1959** Blake Stone *Widow's Cruise* 29 Jonas, bringing them finally to the levy and the small shoreline temple, eyes her across the lawn, standing windward toward the ocean. She screams.

SABORU, vb.

Fig. 25: too small red chairs.

1. A single sheet of paper that reads, "Ms. Kristen. I'm Absent. I must go back Home. Bob"
2. Do you like Chicken? Do you like...curry rice? DO you LIKE HAM?! Do you like SUSHI!!!!! DO YOU LIKE NATTO?!
3. This is a key of the shutter box at first floor. Cloud you keep it locked? Thank you very much.

SABOTEN, *n.*

Fig. 26: the third train.

1. Cactus.
2. Please purchase a small cactus at *Humpty Dumpty Department Store* and pretend that it's from the United States. If you ever meet Yatsuko and Yoshi Uchida, please give to them from me. They will make you plenty of fish, peanut butter, oreos, organic corroquet.
3. The eki at the west side of the Japanese Alps reminds you of nothing. It is similar, though, and Yoshi and Yatsuko descend from a silvery SUV to greet you, take your bag and cactus, and drive you to the international artist cabin community they summer in. Ohayo gozaimasu, Ohayo.
See also: peanut butter sandwiches with salmon

SADO, *n.*

Fig. 27: power line bingo maps a sagging route. A particularly good-looking Nihonjin.

1. Tea Ceremony; Krayon preschool
2. After the preschool Jonas drives you in a white jelly bean to the other side of the island. The waterfall there is one he had found for her. You are unsure now how you managed to photograph yourselves so completely. Unsure how he has already forgotten how much you dislike the obvious and overbearing sublime.

1812 Shinohara-san *Diary* (1861) I. 250 powdered and whisked into hot foam, Wetzeru says, maybe it's like the sacrament. **1844** J.F. Smithwicks *Leaves & All.* xxxvi, foamed, tea'd, and sugar-caked. **1888** Hamber Linn Stephens *Teaching Sugei* (1895) II. 386 Her roommate joins them later in a used kimono and geta. She and Jonas are given the most beautiful cups, handed the proper direction, motioned at with two hands like a drink. Roommate replaces an escaped strand of her red hair. Introduces herself.

See also: unnecessary photographs of people you will never see again under any circumstance. See also: that damn embarrassing

picture of you, overexcited to meet the other gaijin on the island.
See also: jonas and his bloodshot eyes.

SAGASU, *v.*

Fig. 28: bus number 77 to the kuwae stop, happy American town.

1. Look for the dress store in the neighboring town. Every month a different color wedding dress, and on the beach, a bride in a daffodil gown.

2. The face of the beach, kotohiki and the temple benches in wood. Where are you from? How do you learn so much Japanese? and Would you like a ride home? He asks you for your phone number and for the first time you are unsure whether or not to give it to him, whether you should take the ride, let him see where you live, the school where you work, the sliding doors.

3. When you get to Okinawa, look for the kanji that spell "Kuwae." This translates to scary, or, upon checking the dictionary, absolutely nothing, and is pronounced like the coo of a mourning dove resting on a plaid bus seat.
    See also: an iPod on repeat, the heat of the day forcing you into
    sleeveless shirts.

SAHO, *n.*

Fig. 29: town hall.

1. Etiquette

2. Manners; *Yes, yes, you are a good tryer! Sugoi! Try this kind*, she carefully places a small dish of gratin with *seashells* next to your chopsticks. *See this boy? Yes, he is very strange. Will only eat from MiniStop! Can you understand? Only likes cola and candy bars and crackers, like that, it's very bad for them.* Suddenly, the Mayor of Kanonji. Suddenly the lazy susan with squid, soba with raw egg, seaweed salad, fish eggs, fermented bean paste, fruit. Suddenly applause.

SAI, *n.*

Fig. 30: an electronic garage door painted mauve featuring a south/east/asian genie-turned-mermaid. Neotenous features.

1. There is at least one entire street of closed shops. She imagines she'll walk here a little earlier in the day, catch the store owners before they close and key up, but tomorrow it's 2:00 pm and abandonment is everywhere except for the tea shop in the center.
2. A bridge over the ravine.
3. Ability; talent. He compliments her as much as he knows how. How can she understand so much Japanese, perhaps he wants to show her the flip side of the gigantic, sandsculpted coin fenced against the ocean. Perhaps he'd like to offer her a ride home.

SAIBU, *n.*

Fig. 31: english sign for locker rental and afternoon ice cream. closed.

1. Details;

1841 Johnson, T.C. *Nonconf.* I. 1 They waged details at each other, waded in slow words. Sometimes he held her hair. Sometimes he'd go to the store for oreos, milk and ice cream, and run the blender despite the sleeping housemates. **1842** J.G. B. Wetzeru *Introd. Clarke's Walks.* 85 The Japanese are nothing if not detail-oriented. In American Happy town, Okinawa-desu! the only A&W for thousands of miles in any oceanic direction, a rootbeeru float conjured behind the counter includes 1. Root beer, 2. Ice, 3. Vanilla Ice Cream. The ice bullies the ice cream in its cramped quarters. She disciplines with a straw, like this: poke. poke. poke. **1845** Fertenholdt, Franz, *Handbk. Of Prev. Lives* 2 And everything spoken before was carefully recorded, the details of backlighting, the nearly crashed automobile, a package of small carrots kept for the long journey. Itemized with little attention to chronology, she sits in the basement kitchen, rolls the chewed pen between her hands, sets the record straight. An inked and new life. **1858** Sugarshells, I.P. *Hist. of Harbors Worldwide* xiii. 116 blown glass, tiny globes of air, destroy her in details.

2. A fountain made of recycled coca cola products.

3. A red Ferris wheel.

SAIGEN GA NAI, *adj.*

Fig. 32: a postcard of an orange.

1. Without bounds; better than she remembers anything, the ride to the airport in may, it's too easy to say may day, too difficult to point out that those bushes have been trimmed to read "mitoyo town." You can't remember why you're in the minivan. And maybe you're not, jonas at the wheel, the hiccupping, the weeping, the weight of sky on shrubbery. At the airport, they take your luggage and give you a coded piece of sticky claim paper, look you over for minutes before calling your boarding number, but don't ask for identification at any point in the process. Everything is tired. Everything is a high school field trip. Everything is uniform and plaid, and the flight is short, and it has rained the entire way.

2. *Saigen'naku.* Endlessly

3. You find your smallest red bag and open your notebook, ready to transcribe gangplanks full of orchids.

See also: You belong to me/not swallowed/
in the sea.

SAIGO NI, *adv.*

Fig. 33: black on black frost skyline.

1. In the end they had to preserve the endangered fish, dam the red wall of water, wait for him.

SAIKO SURU, *n.*

Fig. 34: a schoolroom professor asks, Is this about a wake? You know, a wake.

1. Reconsider.

    1783 Johnson *Let. to K.* 6 Jun. in *Ivins*, he begs you to reconsider, or to consider in the first place, your carefully recorded memories. You want to ask whether you should remember the polished wood so well? Everything is covered in saccharine scent. You've thought it over, and is he at least in *there?* You'll stand in the corner with your eyes nearly closed if they'll just open the shiny lip over his torso. You'll stand a little closer, but you won't touch anything. You get a little closer and look as little as you can at his face, look again, but don't count the stitches over his closed eye, or the length of his eyelashes resting over such a pale swath of skin. **1800** *Asiat. Proc. E. Ind. Ho.* 82/1 Consider how you'll ever get back from the sovereign nation of Japan. **1856** A. M. Mickleson *Elem. Law & Pract. Legis. Assemblies U.S.* §1264 Consider that all you'll ever need to say, *Sumi masen.* When she interviews you, she'll want to know why you're interested in Japan; You're unsure whether or not your feelings are genuine. **1891** Johnson, T.C. *Electronic Voices* 15, His voice falls over the side of your cheek like water clouding the inside of a glass, each word a crystalline constellation of condensation: the ethereal map
    ready to evaporate at your first hesitation.

2. Reexamine. Everything you've seen was through a microscope.

SAIKU SURU, *vb.*

Fig. 35: email inboxes.

1. Devise;
2. Manipulate;

    See also: to take advantage of; taking advantage of [someone] or [something] specifically in regards to overtime work and after hours calls.

SAISEI SURU, *vb.*

Fig. 36: an incomprehensible graph of this life and the days it will be picked up at the curb.

1. Recycle
2. To be reborn
3. Revive. When she closes her eyes, the figure of a brown bird flapping its wings wildly.

SAISHO, *n.*

Fig. 37: a lampshade with fringe, the television glow of four roommates you've never seen before. Note to self: roommates are hot, must explore further options.

1. Beginning; the first time, she wakes wrapped in his body heat, his hand resting on her left breast, where it slid sleepily from her neck sometime in the quiet dark. She slides it down to her waist before brushing the matted hair from his forehead, whispering for a ride home.
2. Dear Carmel Apple Empanada, Tu es muy frito. It's nice to meet you. Nice to meet you too.
   See also: Wee Sing Lyrics, *This is my mother NICE! To meet you, Nice to meet you too; This is my father NICE! To meet you, nice to meet you too!*

SAISHOKU-SHUGISHA, *n.*

Fig. 38: a set meal featuring tankatsu.

1. Vegetarian; this question becomes increasingly difficult to answer over dinner, usually pot roast, is often translated as *Why don't you like my pot roast?*
2. Chitomi-san, with her small, round face, offers to take you and Roommate to lunch for Tonkatsu, which sounds close enough to the city name, Takamatsu, to make you giggle at the cutlet she orders for your plate.

SAISHO NI, *adj.*

Fig. 39: late night exchange featuring fluorescent lighting.

1. First of all, she didn't get enough change at the airport stand to make the payphone call last longer than two minutes;
2. At the outset she set her red bags on the platform and looked for someone who would be looking for her. In the end a Pakistani student computer programmer found her standing on the platform and walked her to her own hotel. She slept short and in the morning put on a dress jacket.
3. First of all

SAITEN, *n.*

Fig. 40: a yellowing photograph of August.

1. Sometimes you'll open the door to the hot timbre of a street festival at least two blocks away. Sometimes you'll purchase an orange at the Marunaka.

SAIWAI, *n.*

Fig. 41: a hat shaped like a straw boat.

1. Happiness;
2. Lucky, lucky, lucky, lucky!

1857 Shinoharasama *Putting the FUN! in Fundoshi* 406 the stage at the end of the street falls dark with the evening. Dancers from nearly every local bank and prefecture have learned the steps to the new classic line dance. The chorus: everyone shapes the thumb and forefinger of each hand into an "L", then flicks the wrist as though shaking water from the lines of their fingers, chanting, "Lucky! Lucky! Lucky!" **1864** *Mont St. Chanel's Jrnl.* No. 2/1 At the present moment, when everything has finally darkened around the lucky choir, then fireworks. **1877** Shoppes, F. B. *The Art of Cultural Criticism* 20 Platforms of cheap wood are nailed together into loose boxes, open porches that are hauled out by the men in July. They will dress by simply wrapping a kitchen hand towel around and then between the buttocks, then carry the platforms out to the city center for the festival. **1909** *Englishwoman* Apr. 298, She looks at them, their muscular buttocks flexed. *Callipygian* she'll record later that evening in her diary. The air is hot and heavy with lucky sweat. She's too shy, but she'd like a ride in your platform, onegaishimasu, and she's shoved into the wooden pen and thrust into the sky.

SAIWAI, *adj.*

Fig. 42: curry rice, kare raisu.

1. happy

SAIZEN, *n.*

Fig. 43: the numbers 501 soldered to a heavy door.

1. Best effort;
2. *Saizen o tsukusu.* Put forth one's best effort. In the morning she manages to flood the apartment, break the rice cooker, start her first course over 20 minutes late, and misidentify Akira as a handyman. *See also: Mitsukoshi and the scarves you'd very much like to buy.*

SAKE, *n.*

Fig. 44: a tower of glass at the ¥100 Shop.

1. Japanese white rice wine.
2. alcoholic drink; *you are not interesting at all in this?*

SAKI NI, *adv.*

Fig. 45: a white car in the shape of a jelly bean zips toward the school yard where you are waiting with the peach Calpis you thought she might like.

1. Ahead; formerly
2. *Saki ni iku.* Precede
3. *Prep.* Before, beyond;

SAKKA, n.

Fig. 46: a lamp.

1. Writer

SAKKAKU, n.

Fig. 47: a glass case, a meeting.

1. Illusion; An underground food court with large tiled floors features sealed glass cases of plastic food. Plastic scrambled eggs, plastic curry, plastic gratin, plastic puff pastry, plastic ice cream, plastic shrimp, plastic udon with soup, plastic soba, plastic fish heads, plastic rice, plastic fruit cups, plastic sushi, plastic beer, plastic unidentifiable bowl food, plastic unidentifiable plate food set, plastic spaghetti, plastic toast, plastic parfait with plastic corn flake topping. Point to your lunch!
2. Misunderstanding

SAKUBUN, n.

Fig. 48: a whole room of socially anxious adults.

1. Composition; she reads e.e. cummings, reasoning that everything in this country is an extended metaphor. nothing needs capitalization as much as urgency. if only there were little lights we could hang.
2. I carry your heart. I carry it in my heart. Not as the world carries your heart do I carry your heart. Let your heart not be troubled. Neither let it be carried over the water.

SAKUNEN, n., adv.,

Fig. 49: a canvas taken out of the plastic wrap.

1. Last year
2. Everything occurs in ones. At this time last year you were asleep. At this time last year you stopped eating. At this time last year you picked out your first black dress. At this time last year the sun burned your neck. At this time last year, the wrinkles in your face began to set, and for the first time, you aged.

SAKURA, *n.*

Fig. 50: live through this and you won't look back.

1. Cherry Tree;
2. Cherry Blossom
3. She lets the car idle while she tells you that everything is for the best in this tiny light.

SAKURAMBO, *n.*

Fig. 51: tenmaya; ferri-dori.

1. A platform of the tennis shoes one might find on a fleet of old, small women, an escalator to the ¥100 shop. Umbrella stands and fans and a rack of scarves and vacuum cleaners and upstairs but to the right is where you can find a summer yukata with the prettiest sash.

SAKUSHA, *n.*

Fig. 52: konami-chan at the helm of the organ.

1. Writer; author; creator;
2. Children fold better cranes than you do.

-SAMA,

Fig. 53: a cement room with a space heater on either side of the rows of metal folding chairs.

1. Mr.; Mrs.; Ms.; (formal)
2. Dear Mr. God, (this is how we pray), would you please look at me. just. look.
3. She wonders how any of this is translated. And then they ate cold, summer udon with chopsticks and drank the broth from the side of the paper cup, and it was hard.

SAMASU, *vb.*

Fig. 54: plaid twin sheet set.

1. She wakes up too hot to his hand sweeping her hair back behind her ear. He's saying something so quietly. He falls her back to sleep.
2. She wakes up and again he's already looking at her, this time from the twin mattress they dragged in. She pulls her hair up and asks what he would have for breakfast if he could have anything. Except for eggs, which she doesn't know how to make. She stands at the stove in her satin & cream colored pajamas, his sweater pulled over her top, cracking eggs into a bowl for French toast. They talk about getting tickets to the game. His arm slides around her waist. His sister calls. For the last time, everything is the way it should be.

SAMERU, *vb.*

Fig. 55: a white board.

1. Lose color.
2. The weekly office meeting is held in the second room, partitioned from the games by a folding wall. We are sitting in primary colored chairs around a table when Meme comes in, hiccupping, tearing over, and we are made to feel it is our fault. We have been bad, but no one can figure out exactly what has happened.
   See also: bookshelves stacked haphazardly along the back wall, underneath a plethora of squishy toys for safety.

-SAN,

Fig. 56: a stained mouth.

1. Mr., Mrs., Ms., and remember to shave your upper lip. Her boss says *I hope it's not rude. Is it rude to say shave your upper lip?*
2. Kuchi-san; Ms. Mouth. Ryo wears dark glasses inside and won't turn on the aircon because you can hear it behind the camera. In Japanese: You *look like a psychopath with all that lipstick on. No she doesn't. kowai ne?*
3. Ms. Mouth, Ms. Lips, they've never seen lips like yours in real life and when the children touch the electronic pen to the pad, a close up of your mouth saying, "Lips! Lll Iii Pp Sssss. Lips!" plays on a tiny

computer screen. Her mouth becomes a registered trademark and she's forced to pay royalties per syllable uttered.

SANPO SURU, *vb.*

Fig. 57: raked gravel in squares.

1.   Go for a walk; Everything in this house is painted in gold leaf. Except the back door, which everyone keeps photographing, the flash strobe-lighting. A hurried pulse. You've run around me in circles in every town on this island; a wake of winded leaves dusts my hair, sticks to my sweater and socks. I almost always find you on a rooftop at the ringing of the bell.

SAPPARI, *adj.*

Fig. 58: a knot, an obi.

1.   Not at all;
2.   *Sappari wakaranai.* I don't understand at all. *We think he's gone. We think.*

SARADA, *n.*

Fig. 59: a single, ripe cherry tomato escapes to the side of a fork.

1.   Salad; [at the burger palace] *I'm a vegetarian,* she says, *watashi-wa begitarian desu.* [blank] [stare].

SASHIMI, *n.*

Fig. 60: a platter.

1.   As long as it's not moving anymore, she says.
2.   Conveyered fish on plates circle the room like tiny sharks on a track. She never really learns what words like "unagi" mean, but quickly recognizes edible from rubber and ferment. The only thing the white girls will teach her is arigato gozaimasu, arigato gozaimashita, teaching her to overthank for everything.

SASSURU, *vb.*

Fig. 61: two pockets.

1. Guess; imagine
2. Sympathize
3. Mm, mm, mm mm mmm mm mm.

SASSURAI, *vb.*

Fig. 62: a torii at high tide.

1. Wandering. The orange rolls itself perpendicular to its little apartment on the ravine, stops at the ocean, and slides its tiny headphones over its navel. *Listen to this*, she says to the dormant seeds. *Listen to the gulls, how they weep.*

SATO, *n.*

Fig. 63: a stone building north; a stone building south.

1. Hometown. *Disney Lando is here*, she points to the mothers of 3 eager 8-year-olds, *and* here *is where Disney Worudo is.*

SAZUKERU, *vb.*

Fig. 64: the accordion platform from port to plane.

1. To give; grant. Miyuki gives her time off; three days of rain on the birth island.

SHI, *n.*

Fig. 65: the figure of every homonym for the following words.

1. Four
2. Death
3. Poem

SHIBARAKU, *adv.*

Fig. 66: a bridge for rowing races.

1. For a while; for a long time;
2. She wakes to find the whole thing a terrible joke. He's been found by the side of the road or the river and cannot remember her. His left arm withered and limp, hangs to the side of his now misshapen (waterlogged) torso. He holds her with his good arm and she breathes in the scent of his broken collarbone, weaves her fingers through his hair. But what was he doing by the road. Sometimes his eyes are blank for her. Sometimes they flash with recognition. She wears her best red lipstick. She wakes to find the whole thing a terrible joke.

SHIBO, *n.*

Fig. 67: The Love for Three Oranges Internet Broadcast.

1. The curator calls from southern Utah where they've been, as they say, recreating. Recreating the fall.
2. The curator calls from southern Utah while she was out. Memorial Day is for recreating.
3. The curator calls from southern Utah and leaves a hurried message to call back because our protagonist was out recreating and now she's on her way home.

4. The curator answers from southern Utah and says there's been a fall. That man might have sorrow. That man might have recreation.
5. The curator says in southern Utah there's a waterfall waterslide flood year. That man might have fallen.
6. The curator says in the flood year southern Utah is the color of sun, a baptism by water, by fire, that man might fall.
7. The curator slumps by the hanging phone. Our protagonist is on her way home, horror rising the 35-foot length of her throat, the length of an arm lowered into the bath water, the pool water, the white and zippered water, the red rock and foaming water.

SHIBO, *n.*

Fig. 68: gunlock reservoir.

1. She wished a head injury. Preservation in cold water. The stitched lid. The long and closed lashes.

SHICHIGATSU, *n.*

Fig. 69: the first solo flight.

1. July fills her small house of sliding doors with hot, wet air. The inland sea drains, leaves the imprint of a large coin on the side of its bed. The ravine struggles to hold so many turtles.

SHICHO, *n.*

Fig. 70: DoCoMo mushrooms and sea urchins.

1. Mayor; Mitomi-San tells you there is Big Snake in the potted plant by the elementary school bathroom. She invites you to dinner with the Mayor of Kanonji and asks you to please wear nice clothes and looks genuinely pleased or relieved when she picks you up and you are both wearing dark skirts and pale pink shirts. Mitomi talks you through the 9 course meal, 1. Seaweed salad; 2. Seashell gratin; 3. Wheat soba with raw egg; 4. Sea urchin on rice; 5. Various unidentifiable pieces of sashimi or natto; 6. Fruit; 7. Ume-boshi; 8. Corroquet in curry; 9. Anko Mochi; and you are a good tryer! The mayor is a large-ish politically greasy man. He is pleased to meet you, pleased to meet you too, and this is my gift to you for teaching

English in Kanonji – he carefully removes the plastic smiling DoCoMo mushroom from the toggle of his cell phone and ceremoniously gifts it to you with both hands, bowing low. You sense some insincerity in the length of this presentation but accept his leftovers anyway and agree to have your picture taken.

SHIDAREZUKURA, *n.*

Fig. 71: a parking lot full of dropped laundry.

1.   Weeping cherry tree;

SHIGATSU, *n.*

Fig. 72: where the hell is he?

1.   April.

SHI'ITAKE, *n.*

Fig. 73: the flowers you always want to buy at the market but never do.

1.   Japanese mushroom;

SHIKAI, *n.*

Fig. 74: an orange book of words.

1.   Field of vision; from the balcony he says do you want a ride home? But you are leaving soon.
2.   Before she leaves for Japan, his father puts her in the car, stops at the gate, walks her to the top of the dam. She considers, at length, lowering herself into the now-limp water. She looks quiet. The length of rope he tied around his waist. The endangered species of fish spawning under their bodies. Three days in a cold compress before his head injury began to breathe.

SHIKISHA, *n.*

Fig. 75: the corner store has ice cream.

1. Conductor. *Kore wa Kanonji-ni tomarimaska?* Does it go to
    Kanonji? One half of the train for the big island over a bridge like
    chopsticks balanced between two misshapen plates. The other half to
    Takamatsu where the small domestic airport waits with four
    perfectly lined gates.

SHIKKARI SURU, *vb.*

Fig. 76: the shape of a plane.

1. Become strong;
2. Get a hold on oneself; Okinawa came on like a cold sweat. Two stops
    from the monorail there's a wet-tiled business hotel with a concierge
    who tries especially to learn and remember her name, which sounds
    like *question.* In three days her hair has begun falling out in
    handfuls again, a happy anniversary gift at the shower drain, at the
    corners of the carpet. She spreads the year-old pictures of him in
    order on a double bed that nearly fills the entire room. The archive
    lies quietly next to her until the morning he drowns in again. The
    rain shifts uncomfortably down the window, settling its tiny falls
    against the landscape of his birth and early childhood. She flips his
    old United States Uniformed Services Identification and Privilege
    Card over: Date of Birth: January 5, 1982, Place of Birth: Camp
    Kuwae, Japan, Medical/Civilian, Expiration Date. They had argued
    over whether or not to come here, married or unmarried, and if not,
    how would they ever manage to live alone on an island without
    screwing up their lives. She didn't know. And what to do now that
    she was here with this body of film and paper; Find the beach, stand
    outside the chain link fence and imagine the inside of an old
    hospital, watch the Air Force fly their planes on and off the side of
    the island.

SHIKYU, *n.*

Fig. 77: a college roommate walks you through the door of an unfamiliar apartment, where waiting in the back is everything that was extracted.

1. Uterus;
2. For a long time her sleep is featureless, blank and necessary. She imagines him like a pillow pressing on her low back and this culls something. Spiders touch their tiny teeth to the skin of her torso, and whether or not they are fighting, she can't tell.
3. She's found him by the side of the road they're late for the prom, but shouldn't we stop here for dinner first? A Dinner Party? Yes. Yes, of course we should, and there are clear plastic cups like petri dishes passed around and in hand, yes of course I'll hold her for a moment while / T—, could you hold her for a moment, but she looks so very much like you? Whose baby is this anyway, where did you get this baby, WHOSE BABY? Suspicion directed at her womb.

SHIKYU, *adv.*

Fig. 78: nesting luggage.

Immediately; Meme calls long distance to ask, can you please come to Japan this week. **1827** A. M. Mickleson *Interviews & Exchanges* 27 ...the smaller of the two islands is located immediately south and can be reached via train. **1873** *Nippon: Land of the Rising Tides* January 176 shorelines are netted immediately for the greatest and most thorough catch. **1897** Shellings *Manual of Logic* xii the immediacy of red luggage on a platform demands several loudspeaker announcements translated roughly as, "Has anyone lost their newly landed gaijin?" or "Will the party responsible for a terrified blonde nervously drinking grape soda please come to the information desk for retrieval?" At length, she's led to a hotel, finds a tiny room and another set of train tickets. The guy who helps her says not to worry, that he will sleep in a book store or a coffee shop in a chair because he's missed the last train home, and you've read about this, but this early in the game you're really not sure whether you're supposed to feel guilty or not. You do, but really the situation is helpless.

SHIMA, *n.*

Fig. 79: an olive, pressed.

1816 Black, M. *Open Parks* I. iv. 86 A listing of ferries from Takamatsu to the many nearby islands, most notably Shodoshima, or the Isle of Olives, where a considerable effort to recreate ancient Greek architecture has come to fruition. **1825** Keaning *Let.* 21 Apr. 19, Only I am on this island now. **1896** J. Shurtliff *Island Transport* I. vii. From the port one might select modes of transport varying from the newly instated bus system, to the more primitive and refreshing form of cycling round the island. A combination of busing, cycling and walking is recommended for viewing the narrow straits and the closest set islands in the world. **1901** Mitsumi Tashima [trans.] *Local Directions* ...two American women entered the shop, stumbled over the stuffed animal display of Hello Kitty Heads, and after righting the situation, they smoothed their shirts and pointed to a map with a single word, "Doko?" I replied, "Koko," meaning *here*. The World Record Holding strait was simply around the corner. They might have fallen in, had they continued ten yards in the direction they were already headed. **1910** *Captains* IIV. 293 Spotted! A class of white Americans wearing headbands. They are notably speaking English on the bus and the man with them appears to be the most handsome of our 7-month research set. He is followed by several blonde girls who appear to have researched the bus system and know precisely where the olive museum of the island is located. Let us follow them closely. **1911** I. K. *Casada* 37-39 Near what appears to be a rotunda...island gazebo, there are houses for pressing olive leaves into paper...and the purchasing of olive oils, soaps, elixirs, chapsticks, cosmetic lotions, etc. **1939** O. Pline *Men are Human* xvi. 103 This is a set of bent and broken trees. This particular tree, transplanted to the island from the Middle East under a peace agreement, produces the finest first pressed oil. This is a grove. This is where we graft your branches. I am here, in Japan, near your birth, holding the last strands of your passing, and for a moment I'll wrap my arm in a strip of cloth and join my elbow from your rib to collar bone until finally I am holding the body of you again. **1942** Tr. Cox I. *The Speaking Underworld: Island* And for several minutes, he held the island in his large and capable wingspan.

SHIMAI, *n.*

Fig. 80: the figure of a street wilted twin girl.

1. Sister-in-

   1959 S. Green *Only Hearts* 153 'You know, she's really hot until you realize that she looks exactly like the girl version of her brother,' he said, having won the last round of bowling. **1977** S. Winchester *Piers and Warehouses* i. 77 Inside a warehouse remodeled as a bowling alley, several vending machines line the back wall. One inserts the correct amount of change, selects a shoe size, and leather-soled bowling shoes are vended like a diet coke and chips. Lift the plastic cover to extract clown shoes.

2. Sisters. At church they call her *sister* and she feels this could be the small nunnery she got herself to. The building is dank and feels like cement with partitions in the main room. A class for English. A class in Japanese. Shimai, she plays the organ, sings in the choir, teaches the English Sunday School and occasionally speaks, although translation is necessary and arduous.

3. Am/ba/rine-shimai, her roommate, has 8 brothers and sisters and will tell you about them in depth the first time you meet. A great conversationalist, you have a lot to learn from this gab gifted girl. Her older sister, Jealousy, and her younger sister, Cheerleader, enjoy her company equally and she's often needed on the phone that is a microphone wired to her new and freshly-stickered laptop.
   See also: The lack of family pictures in the main album; a younger sister who married in the dead of this last winter; her eyelashes, a broken comb, a thrown box of dried roses.

SHIN, *n.*

Fig. 81: an udon shop on every corner, the first sign you learn to read.

1. Heart;
2. Center

SHINBUN, *n.*

Fig. 82: the set of cubicles where Ryo flirts with a 15-year-old girl.

1.   Newspaper: Your picture is featured in the local weekly newspaper featuring Kanonji's finest: *Let's Try!* puts your picture on the front page, blonde and bunned in business attire, and maybe if you're lucky you'll become the representative Ego no sensei at the mayoral dinner in the end. In truth, you have absolutely no idea what it says and it could be a human interest piece or a bounty on your American words.

SHINCHU, *n.*

Fig. 83: a pickled plum.

1.   Innermost thoughts; Yoshi sits in the corner of his cabin and carves a small wood figurine. His emotionless face betrays little. *In the east, he says, we eat rice and fish, and you eat chicken and potatoes. It's the same, a carbohydrate and protein. Everyone has essence the same.*

SHINDAI, *n.*

Fig. 84: a finger dragging along a globe stops in the eastern hemisphere.

1.   Bed;
2.   The house of sliding doors is outfitted with two western-style beds. One may or may not be infested with mites. She sleeps there anyway, the cold brush of her hand on her own waist. *So cold*, he had said. *How can your waist be so cold?* He drew his chapped hand from her shoulder down the length of her side to her hip.
3.   Graduation from a twin bunk bed equals graduation from the university they attended from the years 1927-1929, one of several where falling asleep in the company of one's beloved was specifically prohibited. To wake outside a chalk circle equals expulsion. She runs her fingers along his arm, asks him to drive her home before the graduation ceremony in two hours. This is how she sleeps: after four years of using the whole night feverishly painting canvasses with nonsensical letters, he holds her until it's over, kisses her forehead and locks the front door behind him.

4. Everything is this tired here: the whirring of window-installed air conditioner will become the sound of a plane landing on his island, airforced and over-americanized and no one will be surprised when she lands. She is surprised by the orchids.

SHINFONI, *n.*

Fig. 85: a portable cd player and the Wee Sing Series.

1. Symphony
2. baby, baby, I hear a shinfoni

SHINGAO, *n.*

Fig. 86: the winter's rice.

1. Newcomer; New face. In the morning there are Henro wearing white smocks, hats, walking sticks with bells, and one of them looks like his father. She wonders about Harry, and whether or not he still walks along the top of the dam, watching everything drop and drop and rewind.

SHINJU, *n.*

Fig. 87: a rope, a rock, a body of water.

1. Double suicide. He asks her *did he jump* and it has to be translated like this: big eyes, quiet asking. The missionaries translate for him, then you, *no, he fell* and then as a translator's note, the tall one adds, *yeah, because who would do that if they had a girl as pretty as you are?* To this she has no response, other than *no, no, he would never jump.* She would have jumped.

SHINKANSEN, *n.*

Fig. 88: a map of pigmented clouds.

1. Bullet Train
2. She loves the bullet train so much that according to Roommate's suggestion, she may just marry it.
3. Roommate gets this idea that we should both call in sick on a Friday and take the Shinkansen to Kyushu. At the museum there are clouds on book covers and canvases, and a chair in the shape of a bird's nest hanging from the ceiling. You curl up inside and swing just enough to catch up with the earth's slow rotation.

SHINKEN (NA), *adj.*

Fig. 89: the keystone orange at the bottom left corner of the pyramid.

1. Earnest
2. Sincere. The smallest person you've ever seen, and like an inevitable cliché, a heart the size of her sweet fist, larger than the sum of its ventricles. Meme looks down, away from the camera, her glossy black gaze running over maps, instructions, timetables, and tickets she would paperclip to your shirt. *Okay! Okay!* begins every sentence, *Mm, mm, mm, mm,* understanding indicated in her earnest posture. Tiny Hero: you stay me here.

SHINKINKAN, *n.*

Fig. 90: a tent, the stakes.

1. Feeling of intimacy;
2. 1927, he tells her that if he could live on her skin, he'd take a tent.
3. Latticed fingers. She laces her own fingers together, fingers the brown ring, the inlaid moon and star. Scrawls on a sheet of paper, *I would give you the moon and a star.*

SHIINPAI, *n.*

Fig. 91: the corner store.

1. Anxiety
2. Worry, but completely blank. For nothing that hasn't already happened. She draws a map of how to get back to her apartment from here, where the school and the train station are; her lower eyelid moves involuntarily. Again. Look at this, you can actually see your eyelid twitching, it doesn't stop when you touch it or catch it in the mirror it just goes about its business without letting you interrupt thank you very much.

SU, *n.*

Fig. 92: the house of sliding doors.

1. Animal habitat, nest, cobweb, den, honeycomb; This house has thirty-six doors. This house has 57 onions with eyes. In this house [of sliding doors] two [glass][doors] open onto a concrete bed exposed to the ravine-laden sky. A rusty drain. An angular drying rack with plastic pins holds her underwear with some trepidation over a bank of turtles. All of this is, she supposes, expected.

SU, *n.*

Fig. 93: how many flags, how many fish.

1. Number of months allowable under current visa: 12; Number of English speakers in the area: 4; Number of 24-hour mini-marts within walking distance: 2; Number of Marunakas within a 7-mile radius: 9; Number of bows at the nursery school each morning: 4; Number of children in each pre-school class: 23.5; Number of pens floating restlessly at the bottom of your current bag: 16 or more;

SUGAO, *n.*

Fig. 94: an eyelid; the back of an eyelid.

1. True self;
2. Un-made up face. Meme says you must see the doctor about this, about your eyelid, which is so swollen you can no longer wear makeup and have resorted to wearing a ridiculously plastic pair of sunglasses to class. The children don't really notice. Meme reads your un-made up face in her first language. She gauges the jag of the skin under your left eye, the occasional twitch left over from the summer you nearly killed yourself in. The summer before you came here. And before you came here, you knew you would die.

SUGARU, *vb.*

Fig. 95: fuel.

1. Cling to. I watch the filaments flicker inside your hewn glass eyes.
2. His mother writes to you in Japan, and says she's spoken with him, channeled his feelings and that he loves you, and that he'd like for you to move on. You write back and tell her he can't break up with you, he's dead, which was brave of you, but you curl your fingers around the telephone cord for the following six hours, reassuring yourself in the coil, how it holds your disembodied voice. The books don't say anything about breaking up with someone from the grave. It's simply not fair.

SUGATA, *n.*

Fig. 96: a statue of two lions mating as a landmark in Toyohama.

1. Appearance; figure; features. These begin to fade.
2. Condition. The condition wears. Your condition wears. His things wear. His face wears.

SUGATA O ARAWASU, *vb.*

Fig. 97: a picture of divination.

Appear; to show oneself. **1559** *Fynn. Mag., R. Resilien* iix, as though she expected him to appear there simply because she had asked him to. **1606** *Works, Gl.,* vi. 16 and when he appeared at the surface of the water, a single gash from the eyebrow to the hairline began to bleed. **1659** *Hentsley, Viewings Verses* 113 At every new piece of architecture she imagined him resting against the sweeping, tiled gables – appearing there, as though it had been no trouble at all to land on the roof, and that he had, in fact, been waiting there for her for some time now. And this is how everything lost its fresh eyes. **1772** *Strollings* 7-9, Sam asks me if I liked him for his good looks or his brain and is completely serious, and so am I when I tell him I think he's ridiculously handsome and I leave out the part about how he looks very much like his brothers and that it is too difficult to listen to your voice anymore. I call from the grass outside the park and when Sam answers I hang up under the pretense of a bad connection and frankly I can't speak to his ghost this way. I wait too long to call his cell phone again and the voice mail message has been changed to something for little Amie who looks like she's 21 and all legs. I wait too long again and lose the voice mail messages left on my phone, sent and stored compulsively every two weeks until Japan. Until I cancel my service. I can't keep his voice anymore and they confirm this at customer service when I call and say I know this is very strange, but I have to keep this voice I have to keep this voice I have to keep this voice here until it's a whisper of itself and I no longer recognize it as my own. **1890** Pines *Olaf.* II. 223 She asks him to appear, but at length agrees that she would be afraid if he did, and settles for laying her hand over the warm place on her shoulder.

Translator's Note: The beloved is conspicuously absent from the country of destination except by divination.

See also: A hand-sewn diary, in which a twenty-something girl with hollow eyes and cheeks scratches out everything she can remember. Blank and lined pages fill with the skeleton, an arm fleshing out, a chunk of scissored hair, a broken collarbone with a perennial bruise.

SUGOI, *n.*

Fig. 98: the following words for when you're older.

1. Amazing. Roommate takes the phrasebook and opens it to the section on sex and leisure and begins, *kisu shite, anata ga hoshi.* I want you. I look at her with mock come-hither eyes. *Sugoi! Sugoi,* which we've been saying to our students, to the ward members, to our boss, *sugoi ne!* She continues, here's how to translate *easy tiger!* I raise an eyebrow. *Chotto matte. Chotto matte? Hai! Unbelievable.* 'Just a minute please' becomes a dirty word. She snickers.

SUHAI, *n.*

Fig. 99: a set of wooden toriis at hillside of the inland sea.

1. Adoration; worship. She thinks to him and she's always thought as prayer, the closet becomes her silent face. *We pray to our ancestry,* Hsiao Lee explains, *resonance.* A stake in our future pinning it to the ground they rest in, over, around.

2. Does this walk toward the end of the island become a prayer when, pressed, she absent-mindedly speaks his name aloud. Did I say that out loud? No. She narrates her life again to her lover in this silent brain-side devotional.

3. Bread is passed in trays to the members of the cold concrete building in Marugame and this takes anywhere from five to ten minutes that roughly equal a small time to reassert oneself to God. She holds a paper made wax-thread-sewn book and inks wings in her best and steadiest pen. This is the time she's afraid of, her lover and God becoming synonymous and separate beings.

SUIDEN, *n.*

Fig. 100: corrugated tin frames.

1. Rice paddy. Jonas and I are looking for the waterfall he knows is around here somewhere. We drive for minutes in every direction along a nervously narrow dirt road. To the side is a rusted volkswagen minibus that has rolled from the road into the rice paddy below.

SUIMINBUSOKU, *n.*

Fig. 101: a map pinned to the wall.

1. Lack of sleep.

SUISHINRYOKU, *n.*

Fig. 102: glass pulls on two closet doors.

1. Driving force: the scale of things to come. She sits alone on a twin bed weighing countries, convincing herself that she's going alone, and for no other reason than to be alone. She fingers a small glass

doorknob she unscrewed from the closet, rolling it through her fingers, between her palms like a clear Magic 8 ball. *Not likely*, it intimates, through the faceted glass. She counters, *All signs point to Yes.* She books the flight. She makes the call. She tells her family *goodbye to you in Colorado where you left without me.*
Watch. This.

SUJI, *n.*

Fig. 103: a runner following the highway.

1. Streak (line).
2. Fiber; muscle; tendon.
3. Story line; logic.
4. Lineage.
5. Heartstrings stretched from London to Omaha.

SUKI, *n.*

Fig. 104: a deaf mute.

1. Fondness; love. What she won't admit to anyone. Anyone can know this, she'd said it, she'd said the word to him after it threatened to leap from her mouth like a flying fish. Its tiny fins flapped as fast and as hard as they could to stay airborne, but when it ultimately dropped into the residual silence; The plaid bedsheets resounded with something like a strung fish making its last attempts at swimming through the air, dumb, strong, then limp.
2. *vb.* Like; love. The first whole sentence she understands in Japanese comes from the Bishop of a tiny branch she attends on Sundays. Something like, *Nippon suki desu?* or the grammatically correct and polite version of the same. She nods and knows for the first time in weeks exactly how to respond, *Nippon ga daisuki desu.* (enthusiasm.) He asks her if she would be willing to play the organ for Sacrament meeting. This is translated as, *Would you be willing to play the organ for Sacrament meeting?* and she accepts, readily.
3. *adj.* Favorite; fond.

SUKKARI, *adv.*

Fig. 105: english type: A a, B b, C c, and so forth.

1.   Completely; thoroughly. Miyuki watches you type despite the fact that she cannot read in English at the rate that you can create and destroy everything she ever wanted to know.

SUKOSHI MO, *adv.*

Fig. 106: the romanji lettering for Marunaka.

1.   Not at all (with negative). Or what everyone seems to think means, "a little bit," "not a little bit at all." They ask you whether or not you know "sukoshi?" and you think this is how it is spelled: skosh(i). For example, perhaps you understand, or not at all. Not a little bit at all.
2.   The narrator calls while you're out playing mini golf in Draper.
     I'm sorry, she says.
     She says, *reservoir,* and some words
     and then *but we think that he's gone*
     we're pretty sure he's gone

SUKUI, *n.*

Fig. 107: a picture of spring seasonal peach Calpis.

1.   Help.
2.   Hope. Sugarwater rises to the occasion as Meme pulls around the corner in her small, bean-shaped two-door car. Everything about Meme feels like tenacity, a small struggle, the late wintering of hope. Her heart, you sense, is a small atomizer working perfumed blood into her lungs. She doesn't know how good this is, how well-fashioned the machinery, and she scolds you for pointing to it. You hand her a peach Calpis you bought from a street-side vending machine with spare change scraped from the bottom of your school bag. She's picking you up from the preschool where you've finished teaching the best classes of the week, three- and four-year-olds who adore you with reckless abandon and you hug them despite feeling awkward about the idea of a teacher hugging students. How to explain: they are the smallest people you've ever seen, and one in particular will likely love to dance long after he graduates. We don't

talk about this. Instead, Meme asks about the day in general, *and how is your heart?* She often wants to know. This is the entirety of your quiet connection.

See also: technical discourses on the ability of roads to accumulate dust in a climate composed almost entirely of water-on-air.

SUMAI, *n.*

Fig. 108: a series of weights and measures.

1. Residence; House.
    a. the scale of the room is small
    b. if the scale of the sink and the spatula is small
    c. then the scale of the cars and the jelly beans is small
    d. and the scale of the church is electric and cold
    e. the scale of the sky is wet upon wet
    f. the scale of the closet is legless museum
    g. the scale of the house is repaired tin and thatch
    h. the scale of the window is tracked and warped
    i. the scale of the rice is bent earthbound
    j. the scale of the dictionary is a photograph among many
    k. the scale of this longitude is a locus of anxiety
    l. the scale of the fish is shiny and blood slicked
    m. the scale of your organ is heavy on my intestines
    n. the scale of the island is the shape of kidney beans
    o. the scale of the paper factory is the scent of pressed rice
    p. the scale of the mountain is deciduous trees squared
    q. the scale of recycling is twice during workweeks for every one garbage fire
    r. the scale of the fire is one loop for each of our dead
    s. the scale of the fire is one flake of ash per square inch of beach
    t. the scale of the bath is one square
    u. the scale of the tub is one square plus one square in each direction
    v. the scale of potatoes is eyed carefully
    w. the scale of the costumes you are literally forced to wear is one per
    x. the scale of the inland sea is x

y.   the scale of the train timetable is one metre by one package of cheese crackers

z.   the scale of the visa is passport pages divided by time.

SUMANAI, *adj.*

Fig. 109: the band-aid closet.

1.   Inexcusable.
   See also: Pink Bismuth tablets, take two or three, depending on how "loose" you are.

SUMIMASEN, *interj.*

Fig. 110: a small guide to speaking in orange.

1.   I am sorry!
2.   Excuse me!
3.   Thank you!
4.   A preponderance of !

SUMO, *n.*

Fig. 111: feather beds, plastic shoes.

1   Japanese wrestling. A few of the other teachers get cable in their house in Takamatsu and watch the tournament for a few weeks. You are undeniably jealous, but you don't want to say anything because Roommate thought you wouldn't want TV in Japanese anyway and you don't want to hurt her feelings. Instead, at the youth activity, you all stuff your shirts and pants with as many of the small pillows as you can gather from the sleeping rooms and pretend to step into the ring with some tragically small Japanese girls. You bump feather bellies and both fall to the ground.

SUMU, *vb.*

Fig. 112: a parking lot full of filled bike racks.

1.   Reside. You decide in April to begin taking pictures of the ordinary places that you frequent, an abandoned barn, the kendo studio across the street. At night through the summer, the chorus of ten-

year-old disciplined fighting breaks over the eight-foot fence, *hai! ha! ha! hai!* They balance their sticks carefully, mark, point, step. A dance for small men.

SUNAO (NA), *adj.*

Fig. 113: a picture of what it means to be genki.

1. Docile;
2. Honest.

SUNDAN SURU, *vb.*

Fig. 114: the smell of fish on the pavement.

1. Cut into pieces.
   See also: sashimi and invitations to dinners that include, but are not limited to, sashimi, seaweed salad, soup, and spaghetti.

SUPA (MAKETTO), *n.*

Fig. 115: fish sandwiches for lunch.

Supermarket. **1943** *Merchandise & More* (2nd ed.) August 76/7 Local area supermarkets include SATY and Marunaka. SATY offers the following: underground parking, a poorly lit and damp public bathroom with a squatting-style toilet, a McDonald's, a small stationery shop, discount shirts and shoes and discount hard case travel luggage. Luggage is located primarily on the second floor. **1944** *Seven Elevens Around the World* 211 Minimarts crop up on street corners like crocuses in season. Seven 11 chains found primarily in Seoul, where most tourists and teachers travel to obtain visa permits. **1959** *The Rural Approach* 25 May 529/1 Perhaps it was a Marunaka on the ground floor of the SATY. Occasionally Tokushima Kyodai would stop in for flowers and surprise you at Valentine's Day. Chocolates for his wife, he blushed, and a net of oranges. **1976** *Islanders* (Shikoku) 4 June 289 The purchased set of hard case travel luggage came complete with a set of Roman alphabet stickers. Roommate decides carefully what word to stick precisely across the balance beneath the handle: I've got skillz, she approves the use of the zed. She begins, "I-v-e g-o-t s-k- and then the dawn: the sudden realization that this language comes with only single eye. Whether it will remain single to the glory of God? But first, she surveys the remaining vowels: A, E, I, O, U, and ~~sometimes~~ ~~Y~~. Settles, at last, on skullz, because the Jolly Roger is in fashion. The stickers are already in use. **1980** *Irasshaimase!* Feb. 6/1 The regular checkers are available Monday through Friday: First, the middle-aged woman who always wears a white t-shirt. Whether or not it is part of an unspecified uniform is still a topic of debate; second, the twenty-something guy who you catch watching you every time you bend down to lift a bag of jasmine or botan lotus rice, or sometimes to get a box of korun furakes. He hopes, nearly every time, that you will choose his lane, even when it is the longest and least likely. He looks down, he looks at your money very carefully; third, the high school girl who understands the most English, but won't speak to you. The Marunaka and every supermarket for that matter operates on a completely cash-only system. You start carrying around big bills. Hard case travel luggage full of bills that you wheel back to the market every week. **1986** *Foodstuffs and More stuff* 190 From the underground parking lot the automatic doors slide open to reveal a produce section plentiful with first flowers and then fruits that you recognize and don't recognize in equal proportions. Most of what you recognize are oranges. Small oranges, medium oranges, in a pyramid like mikan, mikan, mikan, and so forth.

A graph:

mi

kan

mikan

mikan mikan

mikan mikan mikan

mikan mikan mikan mikan

mikan mikan mikan mikan

mikan mikan mikan mikan

mikan

mik

an

SUPAGETTI, *n.*

Fig. 116: a lakeside Italian restaurant.

1.   Spaghetti

SUPIDO-IHAN, *n.*

Fig. 117: tree-lined.

1.   The straightest road in Japan affords us a speeding trap. Roommate and you, van-bound, are herded into a parking lot where the entire Marugame police force is at work handing out small strips of paper. They claim that your driver's licenses aren't valid in this country, and since neither of you can then drive away, you wait several hours in the police station for Meme to rescue you.

SUPPANUKU, *vb.*

Fig. 118: a cluttered office space.

1.   Divulge (a secret); Reveal.
    and in the most tender moment Miyuki opens the palm of her hand,
        I had wondered

    Yes, when I interviewed for this job, I told her. Why. It used to be important

    But I did not want to ask about this thing, it is so sensitive

    Yes, but I will tell you, it will be his birthday and then I will be finished

    I think it will rain this week

    I am sure that I should go on this day pointing to a calendar, and *Meme-chan will help you to find the tickets*

SURERU, *vb.*

Fig. 119: water washed stones.

1. Rub (against).
2. Wear down.
3. Become jaded.

SURIKIRERU, *vb.*

Fig. 120: the shape of a continent you've never seen.

1. Wear out.

> **1961** Belles *New Craft. 7ᵗʰ Series Circles.* 104 Impetus for gift giving is unclear. The two-week holiday points toward a small plastic bag he brought back from Canoa Quebrada. It's full of rings that you remind yourself regularly not to think too much about. You tell him it's giving you a rash. He says everything from Brazil gives you a rash, and that he had no idea you'd wear it every day from then on. It won't last, he says, and he means the coconut, but the nagging sense the referent was mismatched is difficult to dismiss. **1962** *Journals from the Private Collection of James S. Wing* 1/4 It was an unplanned entrance, A trumps everything by announcing a misnamed death. I thought first of finding the ring and wearing continuously from then on, before recognizing the polished surface the middle finger of my left hand. White cut sun and moon inlay. **1963** *Paradises Worn* III. 150 You are the moon and the stars. You write this down. **1974** *Japan Worn Well* II. ii. (1981) 154 Students accustomed to giving every American English teacher a high five routinely and good-naturedly slammed her hand into the desk, eventually cracking the worn wooden ring down the center inside. She considers this carefully and says nothing. **1986** *¥100 Shopping Center Manual (Trans.)* LII. 652/1, It's nothing to be accused of having gotten your necklace for ¥100 when, really, you found it behind the bed before accusing your lover without malice. **1988** *Steady as She Goes* xii, "That's an ugly necklace," *well it's worn.*

SURIPPA, *n.*

Fig. 121: a bathroom with a heavy door and an open vent.

1. Slippers, specifically blue plastic slippers that are cold and to be worn solely in the bathroom, despite the fact that they never are.
2. You have two students who you teach at home and when you arrive they run to the gate in their outdoor slippers, plastic and pink despite the fact that one is a boy and one is a girl. Gabriel and Karen, but later when you teach them pronouns, you learn that Gabriel and Karen are *she* and *she*.

SURUDOI, *adj.*

Fig. 122: a visionary.

1. Acute; sharp.
2. Insightful; keen. (Meme)

SUSHI, *n.*

Fig. 123: mechanized service.

1. Raw fish slices on rice.

1897 *Cuisines of the East* ch. 7 ...filleting the freshest cuts of salmon with the precision of a [heart] surgeon. **1958** *The Mechanized Chef* iv. 172 The routine with which highly trained sushi chefs produce rolls produces nearly machine-like accuracy. **1977** *Slice, Chop, Roll!* vol. vii 32, ...the latest trend in sushi is the installation of conveyer belts in sushi shops. A thin conveyer belt will be fitted to "begin" a complete circular path at the chef's station, where they can simply serve up single servings and send them around for patrons to select from...in essence, providing guests with a live menu that dances flavors and freshness right under their noses. **1991** *The Miami Slice,* "...says sushi is in vogue, and yet every table has at least one weak-stomached order of teriyaki chicken."

SUSURINAKU, *vb.*

Fig. 124: a sliding door, an open porch.

1. Sob

SUZUME, *n.*

Fig. 125: a little bird descending.

1. Sparrow.

   I imagine(d) you with wings and sitting on the sloped roof of the gate, pacing the car through a field of tumbleweed, sleeping in the seat next to me on every flight from Salt Lake to Kansai and back, holding my arms as I slept, but your face is. timing. out. it's not here, there are your eyes, I imagine the color of your eyes and your stunning backlit hair at twilight (sometimes cliché things happen in real life and they're beautiful despite my inability to say so).

2. You are certain that he couldn't have fallen without notice, without it being a sign of the great and terrible.

SUZURAN, *n.*

Fig. 126: the restoration of fractal memory.

1. Lily of the valley. You cannot hear this phrase without your head breaking into the tabernacle choir's full vibrato rendition of BEHOLD! THE LILIES OF THE VAALLLEEEEYYYY! How they grow. Like this: he pushes them up slowly from the dirt over his open and buried dimensions.

七

SE, *n.*

Fig. 127: trying to make her look at the camera.

1. Back (body). His back is facing the camera. Scratch that. Your back is toward the camera, his arms bracing both of yours. He wants you to have your picture taken as much as you don't want to have your picture taken. This is relevant to the number of pictures that will eventually be replicated and left for people to take one, or several, if they like from the room of ash. the funeral lumped in a pile of names, dates, cards, pictures, laced with scraps of ham and potatoes.

2. The part of the body that bears his handprint, seared. sealed. and every time a little hotter, a little hotter. try to reach. it's so hot now.

3. Height (person); Se ga takai (He) is tall. In the city wearing flats, she's easily the tallest woman by 6 inches. This is probably not true, but it feels true and everyone is ready to accept it as fact. Ready. Swallow.

SEI, *n.*

Fig. 128: wearing a pocket protector and concentrating on paper burning in her fireplace.

1. Life. a. a series of things written down, photographed, catalogued and filed for future use. *Colloq.* phrases: *the wire is live. livid. lithe;* a phrase referring to anything you can remember from 1982 onward. b. her father starts at the picture whenever he sees it, which is often. He'll lay it on its face, the back of her head gracing the night table with wisps of untamed hair, closed eyes, chin down. In the background: a long handled net for catching winged insects. c. when he touches it with her eye, the object in the room becomes ash. the objects in the room become ash. poor midas of the dust. shaken out like a rug, the continent goes up in a fine mist. d. the sun backlights his hair at precisely 5 pm to prove it.

SEI, *n.*

Fig. 129: an unfeigned study of study. in hand: a red mechanical pencil.

1. Gender; sex.
2. Sexual act.
   a. He holds your hand in public for the first time at the National Undergraduate Literary Conference. You're wearing a pair of cream-colored slacks and a matching scarf wrapped movie-star-style over your hair. He loves you.
   b. He hands you what you realize now is the matching pencil from a set. You consider it carefully before handing it back to him, refusing to use it, and what you needed it for you can't remember now anyway. He knows you'll steal it later. You tell him that you'll steal it later & he insists that you should have it now. Buy it, he suggests. I'll take a kiss, he says. You seal the deal. The pencil floats in the cup at the back of your desk. Artifact waiting to become ash.
   c. This is forbidden. You are pressed upon to wait and at least once every four month semester a dark speech is given on repentance.
   d. Even now you wonder if you missed your child. You don't remember him ever writing in a book, even in pencil.
3. Nature; personality. You are a rotating pronoun antagonized at every point. Newly single, white, female, tall, eyes one might call *lake* and then might proceed to drown near, but not in. You harbor a skeleton crew, wait to embark embargo, trade your ribs for a title. You watch his family very carefully wait for you to combust.

SEI, *n.*

Fig. 130: rotating kanji floats in electronic script above the door.

1. Holiness; sacredness. Yoshi explains from the window of his SUV nature provides shapes of interest as holy locations for the gods. The face of the mountain holds a god in its sideways w. Maybe you misunderstood, and the sideways w is the god. In any case there's a tree-lined path that you both walk quietly despite the blossoming

Japanese tourism. At this altitude there is snow, despite April. To spite April with a striking w.

2. Saint; *sei Poro ji'in*, or St. Paul's Cathedral in the blitz. It hangs over your bed, black and white and clouded settling ash. A destruction you can run your hands over and believe in.

3. She tells you the room is going to be like a library and that no one (meaning you dear, specifically) should take books as a personal legacy. You've already taken the copy of *Rose* with his notes on persimmons and you fully intend to keep it. You return to the basement for his copy of *The Old Man and the Sea*, which he'd lent to you when he had a tender crush on you. (You're not sure, but pretty sure, that his roommates dubbed you the "not-so-chubby-brain-girl." Whether "chubby" refers to "girl" or simply "brain" is dubious.) Other things you scour from dusty corners: an ironman watch and one of his old ID cards from the back of a desk drawer, a few notes from class, two t-shirts. You'll start your own library, your own memoriam, lay claim to your own pile of dust.

SEI, *n.*

Fig. 131: a folder full of Easy Hiragana!

1. Fault; Responsibility. Guilt without fault. His mother sends you a message that you shouldn't feel guilty for quoteunquote moving on. The message's veracity seems somewhat questionable to you but not to your mother, whose voice crackles with static over speakerphone. You've thought about pushing Jonas under the rug where he belongs, but you haven't stopped chronicling your dialogue like, but not exactly like, this

   I've injured my finger on the cactus.

   Where did you get it?

   Where does anyone get a cactus.

   Well I've been completely delusional for days, like,

   Uh-huh. Yes, well I'll send it right over. Red.

Really? Just let me turn off this hip-hop so we can rest for a few minutes. Does this tiny couch suit you?

> *If you only feel like crying then that will be fine. Come here. Just,*

Listen I'm singing your name through an aluminum door like an ice-cream truck jingle or a wind chime.

> *Look, I don't want to kiss you at the top of a Ferris wheel or anywhere for that matter. Just,*

Would you just get rid of those goddamn shoes?

Jonas leaves his shoes in the genkan like a good visitor, good local, good native, but they are exactly the same, as though your lover is here, a barefoot onlooker. What a mess.

What a mess.

> *I know, I was just leaving. I'm going to avoid you for the rest of the week for this. Don't be such a baby*

Meme doesn't seem surprised when you burst into tears over his apparent projected forgetfulness. Meme knows displaced attachment at the socket. She doesn't disagree when you sob that he's going to forget all of this.

Will you drop me at the airport next week. Half I'm half hearted you don't know the half, which half and half will surface after all.

SEI'I, *n.*

Fig. 132: a still-shot of cyclists crossing the street in droves. Chuo-dori.

1. Sincerity. He tells you the things that he knows about you with sincerity that registers on a Richter scale. He knows more than two things.

ソ

SO, *adj.*

Fig. 133: a photographed interjection; self-developing: do not shake.

1. So.
2. *adv.* yes; so; in that way.

1992 Hansen, S. John *Fueled* 23 The forgotten article becomes *So des ne*, which translates roughly as, *Oh yes, it is, isn't it?* and is generally followed with *So ka, so ka,* or *Mmm hmm. Yes.* Chitomi Sensei brings threebyfive cards in to work with her and practices, what does this word mean? How do you say (she points vigorously to a word). **1993** Johnson, K.D.J. *Anal.* I. ii, And so they believed that if they could only get her to relinquish everything from august to the following may, as the pebble they would try to bank her against... **1998** Diste, R.T. *Naming the demonic fish* No. 194 He fell. So. *(Implied question notation)* So you weren't going to marry him anyway. **2003** Southbanks *Titles* IV. xxv, The sum total of what she'd heard on the phone was, *reservoir, accident, gone,* and whether or not it was in that order, she cannot be entirely sure. She conjures a boat, she conjures his father with a rope around his waist, he goes down, again, she conjures the divers and a helicopter if only she had enough money she could save him, she could buy his body back to life. **2006** Chambers *Births and Deaths: A Record of Gaijin Hospitals, Gravesites in Modern Japan* 762 It was in that.... carpeted room. She finds and wears his watch to the fence of the hospital, knowing to expect no entry, armed guards. It was the faces that confused her, the smile, and even more often, the lack of recognition of another tall white girl on this glass-shaped island. They walked by without saying hello, without wanting to know anything about her hair, or why she had come.

-SO,

Fig. 134: the water waving in heat on the road.

1. Seem; I hear (that); *yasashiso.* seems easy. the seaming of things together, nouns and homonyms, like the water line at the horizon. illusory. Miyuki admits that she had heard about the circumstances ("the Circumstances") but had not wanted to intrude (a first) or ask too many sensitive questions. (You're willing to concede that this is more sensitive than being asked to wax your upper lip.) She's willing to give you a few days off to visit Okinawa, where he was born. You're willing to go even if she doesn't grant you any time off. It seems difficult to get there, to take the train to the small bus to the airport in Takamatsu for your domestic flight. Everything is a terminal, terminus, an ending point, but nowhere to stay.

SOBA, *n.*

Fig. 135: a slender chopping knife and a very carefully placed knuckle.

1. Buckwheat; buckwheat noodles. Somen.
2. Somen hang from 5-foot racks to the floor like a woman's wheat-colored hair in a perfect comb, perfectly straight. You'd want to run your fingers through it with the timbre of a harpist, strum and pluck each noodle to test its resilience. They hang close under olive trees brought to Shodoshima from, as you recall, Jerusalem. There is something in this, but you aren't sure what.

SOBAKASU, *n.*

Fig. 136: pale hair, pale eyes.

1. Freckles. Miyuki and Ryo ask you to drive cars on the beach for the PENglish project they've been working on. You agree to a day on the beach and when Roommate and you arrive, a woman in a floor-length emerald ball gown is standing, shading herself with a matching parasol. She is having her pictures taken with her new fiancé in front of the ocean. The green of her dress matches nothing but the parasol.

SOBETSUKAI, *n.*

Fig. 137: a hand-drawn pig on a tiny pink pocket.

1. Farewell party. Megume by far tries the hardest to make the time the teachers spend here a cultural experience. Her teachers wear full kimono she chooses and ties for them. She will serve tea to you on tatami. You wear a skirt. You wore a skirt.

SOCHO (NA), *adj.*

Fig. 138: the wooden torii.

1. Solemn. They ask you if you want to go in a limo, and you do because you've never been in a limo before and you've always wanted to go in one and if they ask you it means you're one of the important people at the funeral. You don't want to go. You change your mind. You want to be invited, but ultimately, you choose to drive behind the hearse, despite the fact that no one, not even the limo driver knows how to get to the Ivins City Cemetery. You're not totally sure that's what it's called, but that's close enough for right now.

2. It rains the entire time you're in Okinawa. You're told it's a bad time for travel. You think that a bad time is appropriate and everything on this island knows it.

3. They line the sides of the hole with Astroturf. It's like a bathtub of green easter-egg plastic grass. It's like an open grave with a closed casket.
   His awkward cousin, who you recognize but can't remember her name, she looks at you, and she has a rose in her hand. She approaches you and you think she's wearing a white shirt but you can't remember. She gives you the rose she has in her hand, so you can place it on the casket, a peace rose, the rosebush on his parents' porch. Only longstem.

4. The bus stop across the street. From here you can see Camp Kuwae laced in wire, a snack stand boarded for the winter, a Ferris wheel. The kanji is utilitarian and the memory of this place is gray and spotted with chain-link/barbed wire in bracing curlicues.

5. There is a green tent and you spend some time under it to escape southern Utah's oppressive heat. Everyone closes their eyes while the casket is lowered because this is what is done and when you open

71

your eyes you feel tricked. YOU FEEL TRICKED (goddammit) and
you want to exhume everything from your inside to your outside and
lay it next to the open hole.

6. They hide the tractor that digs the grave's tidy square.
7. But you see it behind the wall.

SODAI (NA), *adj.*

Fig. 139: a box shaped attic and a video camera.

1. Imposing;
    See also: Miyuki
2. Miyuki's presence drives the whole operation. This is not the first
    time you've seen Meme cry, and none of us know exactly what is
    going on in their syllabic dialect. At the weekly teacher meeting we're
    made to feel guilty for Meme-chan's tears; it's all our fault and we'll
    never do it again. The franchise owners line up for inspection.
3. Miyuki calls at 11:00 pm to find out something about the school. For
    the first time you decide not to answer the phone. She calls at least
    five times. You put your foot down.
4. Miyuki sets up the bank accounts and tells you that your first and
    last month's pay will be deposited before you leave. The day before
    you leave your bank account is still empty. So are everyone's threats.

SODAN, *n.*

Fig. 140: the color of Meme's eyes.

1. Advice; consultation.

    Meme, she says, *I would like to go to Okinawa. This is as clear as I
    can be.*

    mmm, mm, mm, nodding, nodding, Meme says
    *I would like to fly on this date. I would like to come home on this
    date. This is the anniversary. This is the date*

    Do you know how to go to Takamatsu?

    Can you draw a map?

O! kay! Okay! Yes.

Meme, do you know tan-jo-bi.

mm, mm, m, Meme holds the phone, slides a piece of paper across the table, deciphers the pictures on the timeline. *You will go in January, I think it maybe will rain, I think it's a time for rain*

SODO, *n.*

Fig. 141: playing all the mini golf you want to, unless you already have.

1. Turmoil; uproar.
2. A missed phone call; the face of her phone lights in a circular pattern. This is what she can hear:
3. Mini golf. I think we should mini golf today, and you spend the day convincing your brothers that they're great mini-golfers, even if they do need two strokes over every hole. You're not any better. You become what you like to call the "Champions of Two." And this has nothing to do with anything other than to say that ordinariness happens nearly every day, you are not beautiful, and then, when it may or may not have started to rain you notice a missed call.
4. Turmoil: golf-balls falling like hail.
5. Uproar: a gas-powered mini-volcano.
6. Safely in the white suburban you were so excited to have, and which you now call the U.S.S. Blizzard because it is approximately the size of a white battle ship, she picks up her phone.
7. The gas powered mini-volcano experiences a controlled eruption.

SOFUTO-KURIMU, *n.*

Fig. 142: sugar rush.

1. Soft-serve ice cream. Everything you remember about this place swims in the smell of the emptied tide. You walk around the corner to the Mini Stop to pick up ice cream sandwiches for everyone back at your concrete apartment. Jonas leaves his shoes by the door. You and your beloved are unnamed as of yet. You both will wait for a headstone. Say it out loud, then.

2. Mini Stop has everything from top shelf vodka to onigiri to häagen-daz, but no soft-serve ice cream, and in fact, you never ate soft-serve ice cream in the sovereign nation of Japan.

SOGO, *n.*

Fig. 143: an airport filled with orchid-lined hallways.

1. Total;
2. Whole. The woman behind the counter understands your perfect English. She circles points of interest on the map, highlights the numbers of buses that will take you to Camp Kuwae. You still don't know what you are doing here. You want to see it first and then decide. The seats on the bus are Kelly green and yellow plaid, and you look the driver in the eye at every stop. Fold, refold the map, tick off the romanji version of every stop. Here they have white overhangs, utilitarian kana, and wire-sewn to the chain link fence at intervals is a sign: do not come here. Do not try to come past this fence.
3. It rains the whole way there. The roads gloss and everything suddenly looks how you imagined the jungle to be. You look at the laminated picture you brought, trying to memorize the details, the numbers and figures, the curl of his hair, the temperature of his gait. The whole point was to leave it there, to leave a piece of him at the gate where he was born, but the picture becomes more precious to you, you hold it longer, imagine your wallet without it. Across the street you sit on a weathered bench. You want to go in. You want to tell them you have a reason for being here, and that you're an American, so, you know, could you come in and take a look around, but you don't, and it doesn't matter, the color of the grimy tile, or the chrome wheels of mobile hospital beds, it doesn't matter, this house of ash, this monument, and so you walk to the beach. it matches the pictures you peeled from his mother's sticky-page photo albums. it matches the childhood you tried to log in your memory as your own. the little shin guards and soccer cleats.

she pulls out the little plastic booklet of pictures that she carries most of the time in her new silver backpack. she tries to think of one that's suitable to be left in the sand, to be swept up or laid upon in a

74

few months. it won't stay at sea. she can't leave it on the steps. five years later she'll think, why didn't I bury it, why didn't I leave it there. She'll wish she completed the romantic gesture so she can write it down, so she can own this moment. Now she can't do anything to prove she meant it.

SOGO (NO), *adj.*

Fig. 144: a photograph of a picture dictionary.

1. Mutual; reciprocal;
2. *Sogo no rikai.* Mutual understanding. When you tell her you have to leave, that you are going to go to poetry school, for shi, haiku, do you know it? she nods without words. you speak like a seizure, the words shaking from your clammy lips. *he is going to forget. he is going to forget me.* when what you mean is that the body forgets, you tried write it all down first.

SOJI, *n.*

Fig. 145: red suitcases in the back of a sliding door closet.

1. Cleaning; dusting; sweeping.

1969 Reinsdadt *Principled Composition* 8. Acclimation. She finally rolled over with the sun, which meant two things: 1. she had acclimated and been bitten in her bedclothes; 2. she would begin cleaning in the morning, beginning with her cottoned mouth. **1972** *Motive* (based on the 1947 screenplay of the same title) act II, scene VI. 83 In the house of sliding doors there was, behind a door, a small-ish vacuum of little value to anyone else in the house. You'd ask Chitomi-san, are there bugs in the tatami, to which she responded with her electronic dictionary, "mites." **1975** C.H. Cane *A Brief History of the Breeding Patterns of Mites.* To which she responded by bathing herself immediately and going for a long walk to the inland sea. 19 *Mod.* The spring cleaning began with her own self, her own integral thought process action mode. Yes.

SOKATSU SURU, *vb.*

Fig. 146: water-logged.

1. Generalize; summarize. This is what you learn first, as you begin to dial your (plural) friends. Summary: in the beginning there was water. You begin to say it earlier in the conversation. By the seventh or eighth it comes out like a boulder vomited from your lungs.

SOKO, *n.*

Fig. 147: a map of the island superimposed over a map of a human hand.

1. Bottom; *Kokoro no soko kara.* From the bottom of one's heart. Meme holds the bottle of peach Calpis you bought for her at the vending machine at the corner down one dusty street from the kunita preschool. Today's lesson: Pleaseand THANKyou. They hold their palms up like flattened aortas ready to absorb you.
   She makes you promise not to buy her another peach Calpis, no matter how delicious and how cheap they are. Not another one, she says as you climb into the back seat of her white, jelly-bean shaped car. You silently promise to hold this in your flattened aorta, if you can rehydrate it.

SOKOKU, *n.*

Fig. 148: a still-shot of cyclists crossing the street in droves. Chuo-dori.

1. Native country.

   1862 E. A. Junior *In God's Country* 74, We fast approached a road sign bearing the name Millard County. He looked at us and declared that it was indeed God's Country, and that he would continue to take *The Millard County Chronicle* as long as he should live. Lauren took this to heart and found her way back to visit the cattle as often as was prudent. **1897** M. I. Angleheart *The Mouth of the Canyon* I. 01, She recounts just before he held perfectly still, returning to God's Native Country. **1904** S. Keys *American Girls* 10, I'd happily go for ice creams with you, Cordelia, because you alone are my invisible companion. **1914** G. Ephron *The Georgian* II. 43 You are cold all winter, there is no heat here, not like in your Native Country. You wear your coat indoors for months.

SOKUJITSU, *n.*

Fig. 149: a girl rolled up on the driveway, holding her legs like this.

1. Same day.
2. You promised that you would move six hours south on the same day.
3. And Meme relays for Miyuki, *Can you come here on the same day?*
4. In the morning you packed him a lunch for the road, and sent him off in a teal Pontiac, and the same day you watched everything obsolesce.

SOMARU, *vb.*

Fig. 150: the smell of fish and buckets.

1. Be dyed or stained.
2. Be influenced.

SONEN, *n.*

Fig. 151: a kamikaze headband.

1. The prime of life. This singular cliché translates in a pinch.

SONO HOKA (NO), *adj.*

Fig. 152: a polaroid photograph that never fully developed.

1. Other; the representation of
   a. Money;
   b. Blonde hair;
   c. Forks.

1944 *Seven Elevens Around the World* 566 Once inside the corner store, two cashiers explain the official rules and regulations of the Hello Kitty lottery. It's a scratch ticket, and they offer you a ¥100 coin to push against the card's pewter coating. This service is offered primarily to international customers because they are typically unseen and unheard on the island of Shikoku. You have the chance to win a Hello Kitty mouse, makeup bag, computer, radio alarm clock, pencil set or sticker collection. **1962** *The Small Island* May, 66-7 Natives in this particular part of the country are additionally isolated from outside nations and have limited opportunities for linguistic advancement. As a result, Shikoku, translated roughly as *four countries,* is the ideal location for mutual investigation of the other. **2006** *The Temple Pilgrimage* 289 Henro, or pilgrims traveling the Shikoku temple circuit dress in symbolic white, carry bell-laden walking sticks and tie triangular hats to their heads with a simple bow under the chin. They are encouraged to devote this time solely to the completion of the pilgrimage, and to separate their bodies and thought processes from those around them. Introspection and introversion become partners in this quest for clarity. Ring the bell. When you arrive, Ring the bell.

SONSHITSU, *n.*

Fig. 153: a figure of speech.

1. Loss. What is lost here is the sum of your parts in some ridiculous mathematical equation of internal organs.
2. His room smells like dust.
3. A loaned book returns with penciled-in notes all over the keystone poem, and you rage until you remember that the notes belonged to him, and that they were there before you let her take the book over the weekend.
4. The fractured memory. Fragmented mental process.
5. The ability to control the actions of your eyelid.
6. Event recall in chronological order or with any real precision.

SORA, *interj.*

Fig. 154: the sound of a kendo practice.

1. Hey!; Look

SORE DEWA, *n.*

Fig. 155: a window filled with a hand painted kimono.

1. *adv.* So; then
2. *interj.* Well!

SORERU, *vb.*

Fig. 156: an answering machine message in an incomprehensible language.

1. Digress; deviate from.
2. Miss.

SOROERU, *vb.*

Fig. 157: a trunk full of one's carefully folded things. a trunk full of his stuff.

1. Arrange; prepare. She prepares to leave the island, to return from Nippon to her home where she spent two months about which she can remember nothing except before and after.
   Before was a week of waiting, a rehearsal, a hearse, a funeral, some gas money and then a drive in the back of a Suburban.
2. Put in order; make complete. The curator tries to put his room in order, to change it before it becomes a private monument, and she gives you a pile of papers because she can't, she can't, she can't do it all.
3. Make uniform. She makes everything uniform because it's how she has to do things. It's how her grandmother raked the shag carpet and how she wants all the binders neatly stacked, every other one facing the opposite direction. She wants to tie the loose coffin to her viscera. She wants her loose viscera tied around his coffin. She is a visceral coffin. She wants a sign over his viscera where she can leave flowers if she wants. She wants to leave flowers there to die without being chastised for the waste in the heat. Everything is a waste in this heat.

SORO-SORO, *adv.*

Fig. 158: a broken wristwatch with a daily alarm.

1. Soon; now; *Soro-soro shitsurei shimasu.* I must be going.
2. Slowly; *Soro-soro aruku.* Walk slowly

SOSHIKI, *n.*

Fig. 159: an excavation site.

1. His funeral was in the old church and the hearse parked in the handicapped parking. We said things. You sang something and sat next to his sister's grandmother who held your hand the whole time. You sat on the stand, but when they asked you to ride in the limo, This is no time to feel special, no time.
2. The burial site is quiet and there is green Astroturf around this square and reinforced hole.

SOSHI SURU, *vb.*

Fig. 160: a butterfly knot.

1. Obstruct; hinder.

SOSU, *n.*

Fig. 161: a still-shot of the weather channel.

1. Total number.
2. The total number of dead is equal to or greater than 1. The total number of dead is at least 2, if not 7. Forecast: The number of dead continues to rise on the third day.

SOTTO, *adv.*

Fig. 162: what you say to yourself before you sleep.

1. Softly; quietly.

SOZOJO NO, *adj.*

Fig. 163: a book by the same name.

1. Imaginary
2. (friend). She had an imaginary friend once about whom she never told him. She was her doll, and she had a name. She imagines him sitting alone on the roof now, watching her only when she's not looking, she turns to catch him staring into the sea. The roof, she learns later, burned down, and what can anyone do at that point but jump into the sea?
3. In a window on the Chuo-dori in Takamatsu there is a gold-silk kimono with birds of paradise, orange fanned beaks rising up from slender stems in the floor-length sleeves. You would love nothing more than to wear this, or to see it worn, see how carefully the ties, how carefully the socks and combs, And this is when you lost the car. The minivan entrusted to your care is in a parking area signified by the same scrolling calligraphy that indicates every parking area for sixteen blocks straight.

SOZOKU, *n.*

Fig. 164: a still shot of cyclists crossing the street in droves. Chuo dori.

1. Inheritance; succession
2. Legacy. (a movie)

花見

HANAMI, *n.*

Fig. 1: cherry blossoms cascading toward the base of the falls.

2. A kamikaze fighter pilot; or *what are you giving your flight for*. He wraps his headband tight, climbs to the top of the tableau, takes an exuberant leap.

ヲ

TA, *n.*

Fig. 165: the train tracks that divide this field from that field.

1. Rice Field

1901 *The Powerful Locomotive* 98 One block from the house in
Toyohama the four corners of green rice meet at the train tracks.
White mechanical arms hold the train tracks like a sentinel holding a
book. The little red button lights up when you press it and the
sentinels decide whether or not to let you cross. **1933** *The
Archipelago* June 13-14 The beach unravels in front of her when she
sees it for the first time. Not the ocean, just this particular beach
with its abandoned wooden boat and oil drums lining the sides when
the tide comes in. She flips over the boat and then pulls out her
camera for documentation. This is going in the book she thinks as
she clicks and clicks. The camera clings to her wrist by a nylon cable,
and clanks around her forearm as she flips the boat over again. From
here you can see the train tracks, the rice fields, the road to Kanonji.
The boat was painted blue once. Camouflaged, she thinks. She
squints into the lowering sun.   **1985** *The Field is White* 127 The rice,
the whole island had become green in the space of a month. Verdant
unlike anything left inside her body since she came to the big island,
and then the small island. The doing kept her alive. The difficulty of
grocery shopping [for example] exhausted her thought processes
enough to go from moment to moment. Aisles of dried seaweed
surrounded her like a preserved underwater corridor toward the
white blurry spot that underwater is the sun, and here right now, is
the backlit milk aisle. Remembering how to drive to the cinder block
church. Remembering how to count the money. Remembering the
rice field across from the ramen shop.

TA (NO), *adj.*

Fig. 166: the other, a beloved.

1. Other; another.
2. The beloved. We wring our hands and drive our car[s] into the Navy yard, to prove that [we are] sorry.
3. A bright spot in the blight of your memory before you left for Japan: His father loaded you into the truck and drove for the desert. He said you're too young for this. The color of the truck is gone. The words are almost gone. What's left is the white of his hair. Harry. The timbre of his voice as we got out of the truck and walked through the red dirt, over a wall to the dam. You hadn't been there yet and he knew you should see it once before you left, before your eyes glazed over for the black season. *This is where he was*, he said. He said words. You looked over the edge and thought about velocity. The flood week that had carried him over the edge was gone, leaving any hope of cushioning your fall in enough water to not break anything left intact. You see everything from here. The water filling up over the second waterfall, the happy din of swimmers, and now he's swimming as hard, as hard as.
   A strip of netting is left from where the fish were held back and the fall was dammed. It waves at you senselessly.

TAIPURAITA, *n.*

Fig. 167: a mechanized system of letters.

1. Typewriter.
2. *adv.* yes; so; in that way.

千

CHI, *n.*

Fig. 168: an old Jethro Tull t-shirt.

1.   Ground; earth; place; location. A map through the backland, through narrow roads held in insect electricity. A map through the desert grid to the place he was buried. No seeded grass in the partially-fenced holy lawn; for a long time the ground lay bare in an oblong circle over where he is now. It has been years and the stone, the heaviest his father could carry, is some roughly hewn reminder of what remains beneath. We started to build your memorial, gluing things to the stone. A marathon medal. Another rock. For a little while, an e.e. cummings poem, but the sprinklers were like rain and she had written it in ink.

Ivins. In Ivins. We talked about living in Ivins.

CHI, *n.*

Fig. 169: one package of sewing needles.

1.   Blood; *chi ga deru,* bleed.
2.   And when they dammed the waterfall, his body floated to the surface, the cold musculature preserved. His lips touched the empty air again, the forehead gash began to bleed. She imagines it red against blue-cold skin. She imagines the stitches it took. She imagines she saw it clearly before they closed the lid on her.
3.   Nine months later, the joke that she learns in Japanese about having blood that doesn't exist and also is the name of a prefecture. Nigata. Or a romanji spelling similar to that, she can't know which.

CHI, *n.*

Fig. 170: a woman's voice as it says, You have one. unheard. message.

1. Intellect; Wisdom. *You're a smart girl, you should kiss me.*

CHIKARAZUKERU, *vb.*

Fig. 171: a quiet book left in the entryway.

1. Encourage; cheer up. You can't get down the stairs this time. You ask your mom, please, I can't see anyone this time. You can't speak without heaving. The days are blank and bankrupt of purpose. Your memory holds a photograph of the couch where you sat most nights, and a bucket of blue paint that you rolled over the textured wallpaper in the little room. You bought glass pulls for the door, the prettiest thing you could do for yourself for three months.

CHIKIN-RAISU, *n.*

Fig. 172: the food court: a selection of plastic foods behind a window.

1. fried rice mixed with chicken, vegetables and ketchup.

CHIKUGOYAKU, *n.*

Fig. 173: a mouth full of feathers.

1. verbatim or word-for-word translation; literal translation. a study in the fragmentation of recorded memory as language relative to the demands of grief on cognitive process. when I say
   いつ家に来ている？ when coming home?, I mean when *are you* coming *home* dammit?

ツ

TSU, *n.*

Fig. 174: a new waterfall in subtropical terrain.

1. connoisseur; expert.
2. Jonas views himself smugly as the resident expert in Shikoku-ness. He comes in with a bag full of natto from the Mini Stop and feeds it to himself with chopsticks, the way a bird would feed its young if only it had a wooden beak. He's put out when the other newly-minted "Cultural Experts" ask for help counting the money or finding the bank. *Miyuki just onegaishimases you, and it's not my job, you know?* he says from the couch rearranged across from the television in the tatami living room you share with Roommate. Behind you is a small stand with a landline and an answering machine that no one calls besides Miyuki.
   You pull up your boots and disagree, but the compassion for another lost-non-native-speaker doesn't move him. Your eyes pan out over the balcony, down to the concrete ravine and power lines, and you're embarrassed that you did like him when you promised to swear off anything resembling the quiet man you talk to until you fall asleep every night.

TSUITERU, *adj.*

Fig. 175: a photographed interjection; self-developing: do not shake.

1. Lucky. Every picture you developed before he drowned sits in your hand like tangible luck, a silver print lining.

テ

TE, *n.*

Fig. 176: newsprint on your fingers.

1. hand. the first time he reached for her hand it was to sing at full
    voice to a song she didn't know, a demo tape found in a used car.
2. means; way.
3. kind; type.

TEBANASU, *vb.*

Fig. 177: an egg timer.

1. part with. to part. to be parted from. he had broken up with her
    once. the bed sheets sat in quiet folds around them. it's not unusual
    that she is in her pajamas and he is in jeans and a consignment shirt;
    she never thought of herself as an insomniac, but sleep never came
    without either first reaching physical exhaustion or being held, and
    so most nights he would stay for an hour, then lock the door behind
    him. but the pillow talk had turned to the banal how are we going to
    make this work and he said he was out of ideas and she said quite
    seriously that she would use that little knife on herself if he left her
    on her own. the resolution was an oreo milkshake at 4:00 am. they
    never spoke of it again.
2. he visited you for the holiday weekend, and on Sunday afternoon, he
    clambered into his teal pontiac and kissed you goodbye.
3. the oranges avalanche from the pyramid fruit stand, a waterfall of
    blood oranges floods your ankles.
4. god bless her, that girl who never said anything, but handed you a
    rose to throw into the ground.
5. she makes her way through the sliding doors of the airport, juggling
    three bags she hasn't been able to manage from the curb by herself.
    she leaves one at the door and checks in, the attendants snicker.

TEBIKI, *n.*

Fig. 178: a dropped two-layer cake with whipped cream and tiny fruit.

1. Instruction Manual.

    2006 Goda *Film and Heat* 23 On the 42nd take of the scene, Miyuki plods up the stairs of the old house to the humid and 80° attic. Her son has been filming close-ups of your lipsticked lips pronouncing the individual syllables of words. He wants you to go smaller than syllables, to the sound of "W" or "N." A picture of an apple, and then your mouth warping it into Ahh phh lll. "Mouth" in Japanese is "kuchi," which sounds enough like coochie to send the English teachers into an absolute riot. They dub her Coochie-san, *Ms. Mouth,* Miyuki would say with delight in her eyes. *Kuchi-San? Hmmm? I was like wondering if you could have the lipstick, you know like a red movie star lipstick on the lips. This way the children can really see the way the mouth has the movement of each sound, yeah? Onegaishimas.* She swipes her mouth with a tube of Candy Apple, and after one take Ryo and Miyuki are chattering back and forth in their own sounds, Miyuki making a noise like whining. She can normally follow most conversations, but this one is past her. They stop. Ryo looks over his glasses and says, *It's like horror, like clown mouth.*

2. Mid-way through the filming of what Miyuki calls PENglish, the project that she has required everyone to leap to, she asks you to write the instruction manual. You spend a few days at the computer: *PENglish is a revolutionary tool for learning English from native speakers;* you begin, *Start by pressing the electronic pen to the pictures in the picture dictionary. When the pen recognizes the image, the screen will show one of the following options: 1. A native English speaker saying the word precisely. 2. A native English speaker pronouncing the syllables slowly so that the individual sounds are distinguishable. 3. A native English speaker acting out the word. 4. A native English speaker doing slapstick Japanese comedy.* You get to forty pages and press print on the office computer. Miyuki's English will never plough through this. You paper clip the

native English speaker instructions, and walk across the street to the Mini Stop for a coke.

TEHAI SURU, *vb.*

Fig. 179: the gloaming.

1. arrange; prepare.
2. institute a search.

2005 *Spectrum St. George Daily* E16 Search and Rescue teams from Colorado City have been asked to head the continuing search for a 23-year-old male presumed drowned at Gunlock reservoir where he and his family were recreating. A statement from local authorities suggests that the man "fell over a dam spillway during a holiday outing." Eight-foot poles are being used to probe the area underneath the 25-30 foot waterfall where the man was last seen. A brother said he saw him clinging to a rock just before he went over. **2005** *Desert Daily News* b11 (cont.) As the search for a drowned St. George man continues into its third day, the family has prepared a memorial service. Mourners will gather at Dixie State College at 8:00 pm to share their thoughts. **2005** *Local News KWX* (transcript) 1 On Wednesday afternoon divers locate body of drowned man directly under the falls at Gunlock. "They were going to try and search for him one more time, and they found him," his brother said in a statement to the university newspaper correspondent. The family's funeral plans are forthcoming.

ト

TO, *parti.*

Fig. 180: black flowers.

1. *conj.* and; *anata to watashi* | you and me in a photograph
2. *prep.* with; *haha to* | with my mother while you put on your black nylons
3. *conj.* when; *uchi ni kaeru to* | when I came back home in the Suburban.
4. *conj.* if; *ame ga furu to* | if it rains you'll get the hell out of here.

TOBU, *v.*

Fig. 181: the sun-bleached skull of a bird.

1. Jump; leap. Your face before you do the thing that you wanted to do and then cannot do. You [can't] bring yourself to the rock and water and throw yourself down.

花見

HANAMI, *n.*

    Fig. 1: cherry blossoms cascading toward the base of the falls.

3.   we spread out our blankets and looked for you in the star-shaped cloth of its blossoms. each beautiful in purpose, in white ignited fall.

ナ

NAGAKU, *adj.*

Fig. 182: a face in profile.

1. long; for a long time; *nagaku ikiru* live long.
    *See also: genealogical cartography. From the looks of this map,
    three generations will pass before your name can be drawn in the
    ash.*

NAGUSAME, *n.*

Fig. 183: a small white car in the shape of a pill.

1. consolation; diversion

    1996 X. Smithson *Xanax: A Complete Guide to Anxiety
    Management,* ...cases of sudden-onset anxiety may also appear as
    hysteria, inability to create coherent thought processes. **1998** I.D.
    Cummings *You Never Stop: Parenting Your Adult Children
    Successfully* 106, A storm of blind hysteria. He gets a bottle from the
    drawer by the sink and says in a tone that sears your core, that you
    need to sleep now, and if you could just take it everything is going to
    be fine.

2. The part when your mother holds both of your shoulders and tells
    you that in the morning everything will be fine for a few minutes,
    and then you will remember.

NAKGOE, *n.*

Fig. 184: a ring made of coconut shell.

1. (human) weeping;

93

二

NI, n.

Fig. 185: the bank at the end of the block, one turn past where you last remember.

1. two (number).

NIHON, n.

Fig. 186: word files, early drafts of stories & poems.

1. Japan. You learn this word about 2 months after you arrive. You are sitting in an ice cream shop with an English teacher who speaks Japanese (rare) and who believes that if he is good, God will reward him with a beautiful wife who is both pious and a nymphomaniac. He doesn't bother translating any part of the conversation he's having with the owner of the wooden shop, and at length, the two of you finally walk home. You tell him you only know how to say two things, *daisuke desu,* and *arigato gozaimasu.*

    If you wanted to add to it, you could say Nihon ga *daisuke desu.* He adds with condescending flavor.

    What does that mean?

    What?

    Nihon

    His eyes widen a little.

NIMAIME, *n.*

Fig. 187: a card hidden in a book

1. good-looking man.
2. She takes his picture to class and the adults say he looks like Brad Pitt. Bu-rado Pitto!

NUSUMU, *vb.*

Fig. 188: the blanket that smells like you.

1. Steal. The list of things you've taken from his old room continues to grow.

   A watch from his drawer, a pair of pajama pants, his copy of Li-Young Lee's *Rose*, *The Old Man and the Sea,* and the things he let you borrow that you won't give back, a sweatshirt, a Palahniuk novel. You open the closet and smell as hard as you can, and you think you can smell him in the back, but his clothes were always second-hand. Maybe he just smelled like dust sometimes. The plaid blanket he always slept with is on the bed and it sits with you at night until you fall asleep.

NEDOKO, *n.*

Fig. 189: a teal-colored pontiac.

1. bed; futon.
2. the first week you meet two missionaries who are from California and help you translate when they feel like it. As far as missionaries go, they're screw-ups, trunky, ready to renounce the two-year oath they took to not even look at a girl with interest. They send you home with a futon to help keep you warm, futon in the sense that it's really more of a down comforter; in the morning insect bites well up on your torso. The comforter is infected with mites.
3. after a series of phone calls you get off the train to meet two people you've never seen before in the Japanese Alps. They're taking you to their cabin for a week, so you bring a small cactus in a planter as a gift. In return they set you up in the guest room on a futon that feels like whipped egg whites folded over your old bones. Cacophonous birds whirling around the cabin squawk until you open your eyes, and you don't know how to tell anyone this, but there were never any birds.

NEGAU, *vb.*

Fig. 190: a picture you've never seen before.

1. ask_hope_ pray_request_demand_require_beg_plead

)

NO, *n, parti.*

Fig. 191: verbs in contrast.

1. a homonym for *field, brain, at, for, in, of, on, from,* and *old-style Japanese theater (Noh).*
2. a bus tour of the city with English Speaking Guide!

NOKOSU, *vb.*

Fig. 192: a folded piece of paper.

1. synapse cut from thread. you push your footprint into the dirt over his grave.

NORIBA, *n.*

Fig. 193: a runner in a marathon.

1. a woman taxi driver with perfectly braided black hair

   1976 Alford, James Marion *Historical Okinawa* 178, Learning to ask carefully, "How much does it cost to go to the Museum?" and pointing at the brochure. **1988** Kenning, Lily *The Water* 65, an empty platform built over the water every spring.

花見

HANAMI, *n.*

Fig. 1: cherry blossoms cascading toward the base of the falls.

4. we waited in the sparse grass, chests thrust toward veiny network of
   branches; the arteries fill slowly white, exhale quiet briefness to ash.

ハ

HA, *n.*

Fig. 194: a figure eight on an ice rink.

1. A school of thought on the arts and the implication of sect-religionism on identity and process.
2. a line of elementary students in blue uniforms.
3. a house of sliding doors.

HAI, *adv.*

Fig. 195: a bicycle parking lot.

1. yes; here (roll call); or yes of course, Meme nods, *Hai!* She says in her small, clear voice. Hers is the first face you see in Kanonji; she meets you at the train station down the street from the school and walks you back to the red-yellow-and-blue GEM School. *Hai, Okay.*

HAI, *n.*

Fig. 196: the broken bodies of turtles in the street.

1. ash

HAI, *n.*

Fig. 197: stitching.

1. lung: the scent of a closet full of his clothes.

HAIJIN, *n.*

Fig. 198: a wooden house.

1. Issa's home in Nojiriko is a small wooden shrine with a dirt lawn and a tree. The description reads, "Haiku poet" and commands an annual festival on his birthday. You sit in the Uchida's International Community Cabin scrawling away at a handmade book, writing a

haiku for the contest later that afternoon. The community schoolroom doubles as a venue for announcing the winners. You say syllables they can't hear. You count words they can't say on your fingers.

HAKA, *n.*

Fig. 199: complimentary ballpoint pens and other sundries cluttering a desk.

1.   a damn hole-in-the-ground without a marker.

ヒ

HIKKI SURU, *vb.*

Fig. 200: koi pond.

1. the forgetting like a second death. she goes to the basement and with the light off, begins to write down everything she can remember, the color of his hair: sand; a backlit moment on the street in front of her house: cinematic; his graduation tassel safety pinned to the carpeted roof of the car where a rear-view mirror should have been: pride; the conversation where he had solved a major linguistic philosophical argument: forgotten.

HIRA-HIRA SURU, *vb.*

Fig. 201: a hand-made book with a red cover.

1. flutter; wave; flap;
2. the feel of an airy hand on her shoulder

HIRO, *n.*

Fig. 202: the line you walk.

1. a fatigued metaphor sewn into an old book

HITORI, *n.*

Fig. 203: The American Heritage Dictionary New College Edition.

1. one person.
2. one unmarried person and the devaluation of grief based upon the missing ring on her finger.

フ

FUKO NA, *adj.*

Fig. 204: broken sunglasses.

1. a new name written in a book about someone else. you lie faithlessly
    to yourself.

FUNDOSHI, *n.*

Fig. 205: a ride home.

1. a loincloth folded from a single slip of fabric, and wound up between
    the buttocks.
    you open your door to a choreographed parade. all four prefectures
    on the island are in straw hats and yukata, their sleeves fall like silk
    cocoons below the wrists. night falls with the battery of your camera,
    and the men slip out of their cotton wraps, flexing their lean
    muscles, their only slightly hairy buttocks, for the audience.
    Roommate catcalls so loud the men on stage blush before they
    launch the wooden platforms above their heads. The city clamors
    Lucky! Lucky! Lucky! Lucky! and you're heaved onto the bouncing
    wooden box, hoisted like a white paper doll into the sky.

FURO, *n.*

Fig. 206: a gas lamp.

1. Japanese bathtub; *furo ni hairu* take a bath; *furoya* public
    bathhouse. Steam in an open room. Condensation on fractured
    glass.

HEI, *n.*

Fig. 207: a view of the paper mill.

1. a wall that slides like a door

    1961 David G. Bloom *Anniversary* 104, every wall of the house doubles as a sliding door, a small square with a balcony that slides open to a view of the ravine. The front door, made of aluminum, is the only notable exception. **1962** *Journals from the Private Collection of James S. Wing* 2/4 She asked *What did you do, when you found out, can you tell me.* She slumped along the wall to the floor in between the tatami bedroom and the linoleum kitchen. She opened her mouth and vomited. **1963** *Home Living* vol. 17, June 111 a summer blanched out of memory.

HEI, *n.*

Fig. 208: a stash of clear umbrellas.

1. She told herself this wasn't a pilgrimage, but after 5 months in Kanonji, the henro in their white pants and wind-chime charmed walking sticks found a way to the road. Meme buys her the tickets, a map from the train station to the bus, and the local airport for the domestic flight to Okinawa for a weekend of rain. His birthplace, according to the military dependent ID she swiped from his desk drawer, was on the island, Camp Kuwae. She rolled the syllables over her lips near homonyms for both "scary" and "cute." She clutches a picture of a towhead boy on a beach.
2. a Naval Hospital behind a fence protected by "Japanese Law." you draw no attention around the American base. it's nice, after all, to get a root beer float, and to not be so tall for three days. but you stop at the fence, turn around, and buy a ticket for an empty Ferris wheel across the street.

HEIYA, *n.*

Fig. 209: a new waterfall.

1. vast flatland; plain. Jonas tells you about the water, about how Kagawa is known throughout Japan for having so much water, a small reservoir at the bottom of every hill. he takes you around a verdant deciduous mountain, where you take a picture of a volkswagen van rolled and rusted out. three minutes later he shows you a small waterfall across from a tree house that he found one day in his ex-girlfriend's car.

木

HONMYO, *n.*

Fig. 210: a bird made of popsicle sticks.

1. an office full of renamed people: Shino, Lupin, Jonas, Meme. You draw her real name in the dust behind the school.
2. a year-long relationship that ends in the discovery that she has been wearing a wig the entire time.
3. a series of small papers signed with her syllable squared.

HONE, *n.*

Fig. 211: a demo tape.

1. a bone handled umbrella; a spring loaded ribcage

HON'NIN, *n.*

Fig. 212: the handwriting in the margin of your book.

1. a person in question; himself or herself. an absent protagonist
2. the deceased;
   a body of work a body of found work a found body

HON NO, *adj.*

Fig. 213: a brown sweater.

1. onions hung on ropes from the corrugated tin roof of a concrete house.
2. a woman's spine folded like a shrimp.

花見

HANAMI, *n.*

Fig. 1: cherry blossoms cascading toward the base of the falls.

5. the trees undress in the warm afternoon, unabashedly shedding
   their pink lace frocks, as
   frilly underthings bask in their own sensuousness, as slender arms
   beckon to the softly made bed, as two asleep in the early afternoon.

ヲ

MA, *interj.*

Fig. 214: perhaps the longest driveway. yes, the longest driveway of all.

1. Oh! Wow!
2. Well!
3. The rosebush at the steps of his house interject like this, "Oh!" as she
    sits on the porch, rocking herself into the phone.

    When she was fourteen and sentimental the peace rose was her
    favorite flower, and there it is now, pointing to her wounds
    with untouchable barbs. She ignores it, will say nothing of
    ironic interjections.

    The phone, seeped between her face and neck, lights in a circular
    pattern around the circumference of the face as if, Well!, and
    nothing that is said registers more than this tiny light.
    See also: wolf spiders and the used car dealership.

MABATAKI, *n.*

Fig. 215: a processional and picture point.

Blink.

1. To shutter with the eye or lid, as in waking, which presumably she
    did. It was too hot and they had slept overheated in the bottom
    bunk. In three hours they would graduate from their university.
2. Open. Shut. Repeat. It's hot in the basement, and she can't bring
    herself to sleep in his room. They can't bear to let her, but will only
    say that she should. Contradiction follows her around like the carpet.
    She shouldn't be here. We can't turn her away. She blinks herself
    awake and rolls over on the couch, folding the old orange quilt under
    her ankles, which now effectively has her shins in a stranglehold.
    The light crosses from under his door and inside, a private sobbing.

3. The sliding door from her tatami room opens like an eye into the kitchen. She sits between, balancing on the wooden track. The light crosses from the hallway to this island.

1858 Karl G. Maeser, *Circles and Other Important Figures of the 20th Century* v.1 "Lest the blinking of our youth prove fatal..." **1912** A.M. Gem, *Summimasen: Practical Japanese Phrases* ed. 1 Blink cautiously as to not miss the last train in the station for the evening. You may choose to use phrases such as, "Excuse me, but could you help me locate the last train in the station?" or more colloquially, "Could you please pass the blink schedule? It is where I'm going next."

See also: Chalk and Chastity: a Celestial Combination

MATOMERU, *v.*

Fig. 216: the first pregnancy of a young and beautiful brown-haired girl.

1. To finish together; settle
2. To summarize

1982 D. Curator *Progeny in East Asia,* She says something about honor, in essence, have you slept together. She won't say it, but she means, "Have you had sex? Well, have you?" **1989** Harold Johnson *Thor and the Adventures of the Underworld* vol. II You would remember Thor if you met him. You would, they all agree.
1957 J.G.B. Wetzel *Guide to Etiquette Abroad* vol. II *The Misappropriations of Floor* ...tatami and carpet are ideal sitting locations. See and be seen, or hide under the table blankets, if you must. It will be nearly dark before they ask her again. She had been looking for a band-aid. It was assumed they had been at it again in the band-aid closet.

3. You want them to mind their own business; they want you to mind your own business. They want to speak with his bishop. They want proof that you aren't holding him back now.

4. In the house with sliding doors she explains her pictures to herself, softly under her breath, practicing.

   See also: a plastic album with one 4x6 in each plastic pocket.

MAYU, *n.*

Fig. 217: a black and white dress.

1. Cocoon; And after all you have done, I want you to have this dress.

MI, *n.*

Fig. 218: synopsis: an orange rolls onto the stage, has a bad case of stage fright, stays until the lights go down.

1. Body, Person;
2. *Hitori mi*: a single person;

    1997 Amie Shibatsu *The Single Girl's Guide to Shakin' it in Shikoku* "She waited at the eki for the signal to cross the street, to the two foot patch of grass and then over the coined bridge to the municipal bike rack where she lived. Most days she walked to Kanonji, the cliff side wooden benches, a stone gate, the pretense of a coin in the sand." **2004** M. Sadako Takuma *Gem Nation* Mm mm. mm. mm, yes, yes. Yes, I understand. **2005** Eika Shinohara *Medical Translations* 2nd ed. 330-376 Do you have any asthma or breathing conditions in your body? Do you have asphyxiation before? Can you please point to your lungs on the map?

3. Fruit; nut; *Mi ga naru:* to bear fruit.

    2005 I.N. Forume *Green Buss Guide to Okinawa* 30-52 It will likely rain. After you comes the deluge. From the white room you'll consider the photographs in their proper alignment with the map. It will become apparent, and bus #51 will become apparent but not until you step out of the covered waiting area. This is what it means: for two dry hours you'll hold up a picture identical with the beach in front of you. Up and down. Flashcards of the life you were supposed to have.

MIKAN, *n.*

Fig. 219: a picture of rain.

1.   Mandarin Orange

MIRU, *v.*

Fig. 220: synopsis: an orange rolls onto the stage, has a bad case of stage fright, rolls off stage left.

1.   Try;

> *Tabetemiru:* To try food **1422** tr. *Secret Dayes.* 188 No one shoulde passe without but reyson to trye. **1536** Marion B. Schelps vi. (1550) 65b, Excepte she be tryed she may nott returne. **1602** Philips *Sham.* I. iii. 79 The family you beg, their adoption tride, and found afteralle yer werth. **1825** S. Shellton *Sayings* Ser. IV. *Times of Trial* 157 She found that he had been speaking quietly to her when she pulled herself from sleep, and that it was dark and late. He's telling her how beautiful she is when she sleeps. He tries to sing to her in whispery and tonal Portuguese. **1881** C.N. Nelison *Short Studies* 174.8 The table in the center of the conference room was a seven-coursed wheel. Meme leans to explain seashell gratin, soba noodles with uncooked egg, seaweed and vinegar, white fleshy squid. The Mayor of Kanonji reaches for his cell phone and as a token of appreciation grants her the DoCoMo Mushroom decorative toggle he's been using. *You are a good tryer*, he says, this is for you.

MIRUKU, *n.*

Fig. 221: the color of a bare and freckled shoulder.

1.   Milk
2.   Appropriate emotional responses to the storage, fat content and pricing of milk.

MISOGI, *n.*

Fig. 222: a bridge from the small island to the big island; the inappropriately small switch for the rail tracks.

1. Purification
2. An Exorcism

> **1957** J.G.B. Wetzel *Guide to Etiquette Abroad* vol. III *Japanese Days on the Highways: A Comprehensive guide to Kagawa* p. 108 Kagawa itself is comprised of two characters, the latter meaning 'River' and indicating the strong presence of water in the prefecture. Kagawa's distinctive shape is flavored by the various natural water formations. To your left, Ohashi, Ohaashi, the bridge, chopsticks, a reaching. p. 247...Route 6 will take you directly to a tunnel... from which you will emerge surrounded by the deafening call of spring insects. p. 372...the beach for which Kagawa garners its fame is Kotohiki Beach, where the famous giant coin is pressed into the sand. Most pilgrims begin here, travelling clockwise to the airport.

3. It's nearly unfathomable to her that she, in fact, drives a company minivan.
4. you are all black, the back of an eyelid, I tell you, I'm going blind (this forgets like a vine, green on the brain, ripe and drowning fruitless).
   See also: silhouette

-MITAI, *adj.*

Fig. 223: a mirrored kimono, a kimono in a mirrored window.

1. Resembling; Seeming
2. She speaks to the bishop and reports that everything was in order. The scales leak, but only a little.
   See also: a star launched against itself marks its own demise. Below, a left-over invitation to the adoption luncheon. From left, his mother behind, introducing you from a folding chair in the corner where you were mostly stunned and given a collection of poetry. Next, a tall woman who knows your best friend's mother in northern Idaho, holding a Styrofoam plate of ham and cheesy

potatoes. The houseplants in baskets have procreated and are beginning to cover the earth. You move one to sit again in your folding chair.

4

MU, *n.*

Fig. 224: a ledger for penmanship.

1. Nothing; a hole

1887 M. S. Parks *Living Crafts* 100 The perfect hole is created simply and easily with the proper household tools. Take this decorative punch, for example, and place it evenly over the desired location for the hole. Press firmly, and pop! A perfect piece falls out. **1890** A. Hutchings (Badm. Libr.) 43 You are matched against the hole that could have formed. She asks you for your opinion, whether it would have been better or worse for the other son, his wife, his tiny girl, or for you, and you concede. You are no match for this. **1893** B. House & Doyle *Ivins Plots* II. 41, And while their eyes were closed, everything was lowered and covered with a green sheet. **1896** Parks Country 5, Dreamside we begin to wade through boxes and honey lapping around our legs, drawing us to sea. We hold on. **1908** A.J. Baird *Advanced Interpretations* 252 Her bottom left eyelid develops a nervous tick. She can't control it, and at its peak, it continues to vibrate her otherwise 20/20 vision even when people are watching. **1935** Graves & Longhurst *The Reporter* 28 Shino, Meme and Akira take her to the newly-leased company apartment. The second tatami room has a western bed, aged pink sheets and a rolling rack. A dirty glass door at the back. The three of them together remark how nice the early 70's architecture is. Tomorrow the washing machine will flood. **1971** *Nightly Tel.* 17 February 1/5 (*heading*) The Sakura line is South and Moving **1972** I. Richards Bellevue *Film Adaptations* 67 From the cement balcony, a ravine full at intervals with turtles. At low tide, they align and allow residents to cross from the tower to the Mini Stop and the pharmacy. The sound of junior kendo practice wafts across the street. *See also: Mochi*

MUSEBU, *vb.*

Fig. 225: a gray elevator with two sliding crosshatched windows. on the left, a yellow hand is bandaged and exclaiming.

1. To be choked (by smoke, tears), especially within a closed or confined space; a cheaply tiled box bound for the fifth floor.
   See also: a couple who reads 1,200 cubic pounds of manga per quarter, annually, and ride the elevator for a buzz.

MUZU-MUZU SURU, *vb.*

Fig. 226: a hand drawn picture of bugs, an electronic dictionary spelling "mites."

1. To feel itchy; to scratch until a surface rash appears. It is the first time and her shaven legs begin to boil under black nylons. Within a week pores open at the knees and shins. She starts vacuuming compulsively. Uses a stiletto to draw white lines down the back of her calves.

X

ME, *n.*

Fig. 227: a cameraman, an oscillating fan.

1. Eye; Discernment
2. Each nail on the tree holds a series of wooden panels, some with cranes, or houses depicted on one side, the incomprehensible desires of thousands of pilgrims on the other. The hatobus tour guide explains that you write to ask for blessings, or for writing your wish.
3. A red Ferris wheel waits in the middle of each city like a third eye, its capillaries carrying you closer to what you wrote and abandoned on a wooden panel.
4. Meme. Roommate draws her name in katakana, then again in hiragana, addressing the note for her box. Meme's eyes earn her the nickname everyone knows her by. You'd check your box every hour on the hour for one or several four-inch pieces of scrap paper and train tickets with Meme's tiny handwriting on them. *I just let you know*, she would carefully pen, then repeating your name again, *please go to kokubunji for the afternoon class today. OK!*

MECHAKUCHA, *adj.*

Fig. 228: a row of symmetrically parked bean cars outside the four-eleven bank.

1. A pair of too-small men's boxers and the corresponding dance.
2. [Chaotic; Irrational]
3. A $35 dropped cake.
4. The ability to smash a fist-sized spider with one's palm.
5. You find that your mouth has been open all along, and the sound that happened from it, that sound.
   See also: fathers & foods; feathers in the mouth.

MEMAI, *n.*

Fig. 229: The discovery of what appears to be an American donut.

1. Dizziness; you've taken the train to the green park in the middle of Hiroshima. the ruins hold the grass down like a dried and emptied birdcage. they hold their ruins like a burst vein, a series of capillaries that met in concrete ruin at a single moment. the body of the park lays lean, clothes itself with square paper.
   you share their dead, the shadow becomes him, you built that memorial to him in your mind. he is the aneurism that made a birdcage of your skull.

MEN, *n.*

Fig. 230: a shack on wheels outside the train station after 10 p.m.

1. Noodles
2. Beef broth with nearly everything, and you are afraid to ask for more, ask for less, or to walk past the train station at night, alone.
3. Shodoshima, the olive island in the inland sea, is covered in rake-like racks of noodle that stand as tall as they can reach. orchards of noodle racks drying, waiting to be cut.

モ

MO, *n.*

Fig. 231: every waterfall after that.

1. Mourning;
2. Pigeons with messages tied to ankles;

MO, *parti.*

Fig. 232: a box full of needles with very large eyes.

1. Also; and
2. Even. It was even as this: he held her arm inside her shirtsleeve and then they both faced the air. In the mountains in January it is cold and dark, and there are a few stars facing the open roof of the car. They choose this moment to fall.

   1953 P. Sugar Wells *Asian Appropriation* xix. 7 Tiny journals full of poems. **1971** L. Gardiner *Under the Milky Way.* IV. ii. 17 Spent and terrified transitions.

   See also: an accident without rain, a loaner convertible, in media res

MO, *adv.*

Fig. 233: an American auditorium full of people she should have met.

1. Already; before long
2. Another; more; *mo sanin* three more people.
3. Red ground a silent slouch, sticky and dry under the nail (the digging). But the heaving of the earth against the sky.

MOKKA, *adv.*

Fig. 234: disappearing ink.

1. Now; at this moment;
    a. at this moment she is sitting on a bed in a tatami room
    b. at this moment she is sitting at a desk in a basement
    c. at this moment she is sitting at a table in a bowling alley
    d. at this moment she is sitting on crabgrass where the headstone should be
    e. at this moment she is wondering if she is sitting on his actual head
    f. at this moment she is sitting in a silver minivan
    g. at this moment she is sitting in a classroom of her peers; they do not know him, and this is all she can say
    h. at this moment she is sitting on a pew
    i. at this moment she is sitting on the wooden bench that overlooks the inland sea
    j. at this moment she is sitting near the wooden gate
    k. at this moment she is sitting on the edge of a hotel bed
    l. at this moment she is sitting on the gray beach
    m. at this moment she is sitting with her back arched so she can see the air force practice
    n. at this moment she is sitting in her room trying to calm herself down
    o. at this moment she is sitting in her bed speaking the words, 'my life is so stupid' out loud
    p. at this moment she is sitting under the porch where she hoped she could find a few strands of his hair
    q. at this moment she is sitting on one of her many plaid couches
    r. at this moment she is sitting Indian style
    s. at this moment she is sitting in front of a camera that takes 33 mm film
    t. at this moment she is sitting in the middle of the road
    u. at this moment she is sitting in his chair
    v. at this moment she is sitting in front of her open trunk, carefully removing the crocheted table runner he gave her

w. at this moment she is sitting alone at their favorite restaurant, where she is applauded by the manager for having the strength to go out alone and treat herself

x. at this moment she is sitting across the table from someone she doesn't know

y. at this moment she is sitting in the Japanese-equivalent of a Denny's

z. at this moment she is sitting on top of the dam.

MOSHIWAKE ARIMASEN, *adj.*

Fig. 235: what is later referred to as a "wake" but more commonly, at least to her, known as a "viewing."

1. I'm sorry

MOTTOMO (NA), *adj.*

Fig. 236: a black dress from the department store.

1. Logical; rational; true; and the false application thereof to earth-bound ground-laden repositories and this entire sovereign nation. *See also: white trim with a small, smart bow.*

花見

HANAMI, *n.*

Fig. 1: cherry blossoms cascading toward the base of the falls.

6. she explained this is its beauty, the whole life comes to this moment, short, and beautiful; we watch the flower fulfill, unfurl, and float to our pale and waiting arms, a rest at last.

YABURERU, *vb.*

Fig. 237: the square root of x.

1. be torn; be ripped, the infinitive form of break, to light your splintered bones on fire, to be last seen clinging to a rock.

YAKUZA, *n.*

Fig. 238: steam.

1. The only tattooed Japanese. A burgundy Bentley with tinted glass.

YASUMONO, *n.*

Fig. 239: milk from corn-fed cows.

1. The nutritional value of Cup Noodles.

YATAI, *n.*

Fig. 240: paralysis.

1. street vendor. at night from the balcony you avoid, sometimes you can see a cart with a light. the man behind it is old, pushes the cart, serves up noodles. you want to go down and stand under his yellow, swinging light bulb and see what you could eat. you want to talk to him, but you are afraid, and you don't know how to say, no, no thank you.
See also: Aisle 6: seaweed; Aisle 7: milk.

フ

YU, *n.*

Fig. 241: a square watermelon.

1. the square tub next to a gas water heater inside a room with a shower head. the gas click click click clicks on and the whole room is a deluge of too-hot water.
2. a colloquialism you bathe yourself in.

YUBIWA, *n.*

Fig. 242: a ring made of coconut shell.

1. small moon cradles a star the color of milk.

YURUSU, *vb.*

Fig. 243: a pocket hymnal.

1. to allow grass to pocket up around your body.
2. a vine green on the brain.

⊐

YO, *n.*

Fig. 244: pink magnolia.

1. she holds her knees up to her left shoulder. the pull string for the overhead light clings to its plastic end cap. the bed is cold. she slumps out and pads across the woven mats, pulls the light on and finds a pen.

YO, *n.*

Fig. 245: tortoise shell.

1. your brother's voice on the phone

   1981 *Parks and Recreation Today* 11 Weather experts are called in each year to chart the progress of the cherry blossom season in each of the parks in Kagawa prefecture. A pink flower on a green screen and a flurry of hand gestures indicate the progress of the opening branches. **1984** Young & Landa *Indices* 17 June, 24, but when your dad called the voice on the machine, he said, was the imperial family of the great Japanese. **1997** *Like and As* 104, The whole language can be reduced to two or three phrases that in a pinch, everything is like or as.

YOKU GA NAI, *adj.*

Fig. 246: ramen in a steaming bowl.

1. The island wrapped in a box with a ribbon and a sticker.

花見

HANAMI, *n.*

Fig. 1: cherry blossoms cascading toward the base of the falls.

7. and the nation stops to watch the quiet terror of a fall, the trees' tenuous waltz between death and preservation.

ラ

RA, *n.*

Fig. 247: reprints; a box of clementines.

1. Plural indicator; more than one
2. In the basement of his house, watching chance footage of graduation, he accepts his diploma. His brother watches, watched him go under, watches him walk across the stage, fall off the blunt edge, rewind, rewind.

RA, *n.*

Fig. 248: the remainder carried over in a paper bag.

1859 *Enquirer.* Aug. 337/1 standing on top of the table, and gesturing with pens clipped together at the ends to make a longish pointer, he led the discussion thusly. Where the hell is April. **1896** *St. George Gaz.* 19 May 4/2 a birthday card hidden in a picture book **1907** K. Eliason *Let.* 22 June (1946) post card, side 1: "I would rather wear a dickey every day for a year than go any longer without seeing you," side 2: water damage. **1921** *Daily Correspondent* (Hurricane, UT) 1 Apr. 8/3 How many did you send? When are they going to stop coming. Maybe the post office can find him. Maybe google and the post office know exactly where he is, how to deliver this message. **1967** 'KSL Transcripts' *Headlines:* i. 20 Search for St. George Man enters third day, searchers barricade reservoir.

RAKKI, *adj.*

Fig. 249: a straw hat in the shape of a boat.

1. Lucky, lucky, lucky, lucky!

1942 *Spectrum.* Jul. 337/1 She opens the sliding door to the evening July heat, distant cymbals pull her down the alley toward the garden shop and onto Kanonji's main drag: a stationery shop, a seamstress, a bar, a store filled entirely with leather handbags, and all of this roped off for the parade, obviously. Blocks of people synchronize their movements, elongated ceremonial dance, then break into *Nihonglish* waving their thumbs and forefingers in the shape of L, for Left, or to them for LUCKY LUCKY LUCKY LUCKY.

RAIHIN, *n.*

Fig. 250: bedrooms with closed doors.

1. Guest; visitor
2. In the week of vigil she was offered two dark red towels and his room to stay in, the bed there, the sheets already washed, his things already shifted, the light mainly left on. The plaid blanket they had slept in and his clothes. Everything else, a pile of ash. His father has moved only less silently from the door. She follows a few minutes later with his blanket, curls herself onto the basement couch.
3. And she mistook Akira for a handyman the next time she saw him. He had run over to help with the flooding, he and Shino behind him, out of breath and explanation.
4. For example, the girl who asked whether her boyfriend had bought it for her at the ¥100 shop. She hates that girl.

RATAI, *parti.*

Fig. 251: a group of cards tied with velum ribbon.

1. Naked body; nudity

1648 Gage *Eastern English and Adventure* xiv. 90 It is winter in the heart of the Japanese Alps. At wooden and leaking inn that her hosts insist is a "ski lodgo" the proprietor props herself against the counter. Nihon-cha? *Mizu*-wa? No tea? Honto? **1733** Y. Uchida *When Bugs Feel Dangerous They Stink* (1768) IV. 55, Yoshi, her host, gleefully repeated in Japanese how she was from Salt Lake City – ni-sen ni olympico wa – she doesn't know how to ski! Haha! **1814** Yatsuko Uchida *The Traditional Woman* I. xx, Rotenburo: an onsen bath outside: steaming oasis. She leans deep over the edge and looks down the mountain, nervously wrapping her breasts in her arms. Movement catches her eye. Pan up: two stories above three men's faces look back at her through a window.

り

RIKAI, *n.*

Fig. 252: the original set of worldcraft encyclopedias.

1. Understanding.

    1729 P. T. Niton *Autobiog. & Trav.* 5 May. (1861) I. 246, Breathless, Meme greets her at the Kanonji eki: an open air room and four tracks with up stairs and down stairs. Meme walks her down the street to a garishly-colored and lighted sign covering the English school. **1752** M. Shimaii *Surprise and Surrealism in South and East Asia* I. 22 The Hospital across the street from the school is precisely equidistant again from the house of sliding doors, plus the width of the ravine and a single cherry tree. On a circular couch lifted from the starship enterprise they wait to be called back. The look on her face says, "this birthday is my lover's, and how did you get it?" Meme nods, yes. Yes, I understand.

2. The girl at the raundory counter writes, durai kureaningu, 10:00 AM, ¥950. And this is how she knows when to come back, how much to pay.

RIKUTSU, *n.*

Fig. 253: Ms., the letter begins, I will not have the class today, you are English is very good. Thank you and see you, we will go to Salt Lake City Someday!!

1. Argument: **1880** P.A. Stilts *Bot.* xx. 535 that photo makes everyone uncomfortable, what does it mean anyway?
2. Theory: **1884** F. James Townse *Sugarburns* 241/1 please dispose of frames in the appropriate language.
3. Pretext: **1911** *Encycl. of Accidents.* XXVI. 70/2 you were never part of this to begin with.

RINGO, *n.*

Fig. 254: a story problem involving instruments of measurement and a legend of household objects or birds.

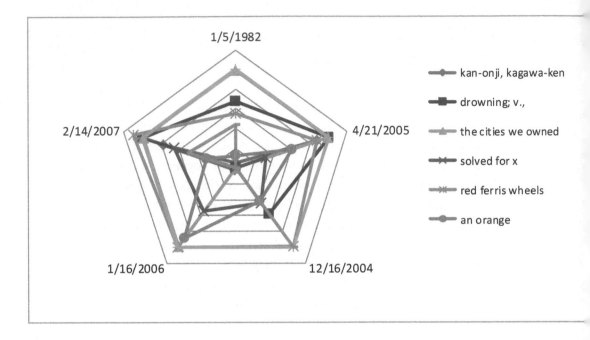

RIYU, *n.*

Fig. 255: the location of the nearest telephone.

1. Reason: *wakari mashta ka?* Do you understand?
2. Excuse: whether or not you mean it.

ル

RUI, *n.*

Fig. 256: a self-inking stamp that features her face.

1. Class; Category. *Gaijin* was the word she most often heard, second to *hello, how are you, fine and you, one-two-three-four-five.* Class was not over until 9:15, meaning they had missed the 9:08 train from Kokubunji and would have to get tickets for the 10:47. The summer air was thick and dark and the ticket window was closed with a tiny garage door. *I love you* and then *hello, do you speak English?* Three plaid skirted teenagers stumble into the abandoned station, the middle wearing a black bra beneath her regulation-white shirt. *I want you I need you.*

2. Type.

    1955 A. James *Fantastic Voyages* (1959) 238 She wanted to be his type. **1980** Sterling P. Pylum *How Japanese is It?* III. xxii. 188 The types of things you might be invited to taste but could suffer [fatally] from: 1. Fugu; 2. Squid; 3. Sugared Seashell. Do not choke or cough up anything at dinner because it is rude and will reveal you. **1996** T. B. Jack, *The Electronic Calculator and its Various Uses* 11-16 he sits next to you in typing class and you secretly practice so that he won't intimidate you anymore. you're better at this than anyone else. type! type! type!

    See also: Town Hall; it's the building with the clock.

RUIGO, *n.*

Fig. 257: the tiniest of Russian dolls.

Synonym; **1921** B. Bergman *Sound & Symbol* ii. 37 Miyuki and her son Ryo have taken her to the beach for filming the revolution. Nearly everything is burned. It looks like a puppet is driving the car. **1964** *Language* XL. 104 The first morning the hollow metal door is pounding. **1980** *Mimeophile* IV. I. 28, An antique parachute; or *give me your parachute.* Colloquial: *your parachute is beautiful and underwater.*

See also: the keys to the practice church

RUSU NI SURU, *v.*

Fig. 258: enough postage and pocket change.

1. Absent: two sets of keys to narrow and electronic doors, the first to a school, second, a keyboard with two pedals and an organ setting for church services. they ask you to play, but you cannot make your fingers do as they please. you cannot bring yourself to take off his ring; the moon and the star.

L

REI, *n.*

Fig. 259: the pictures.

1. Soul. you study the state of the soul in a concrete building that's cold in the winter, hot in the summer. you wear your coat to play the keyboard in "organ" mode and the congregation sings from their katakana hymnals. In Sunday school you take notes, concentrate, make signs of string and paper, draw wings and moons and stars.
2. Ghost. Holy and otherwise. you mumble to yourself when you're not paying attention, telling him about your day in fragments and full reports. you start with God, but somehow in the middle you've hemorrhaged. you're talking to him instead and this innate deification punctures the bird in your chest. three in one, in purpose, or in body, cradled within.

   2006 Franklin, J. *Translating the Holy Word* p 42, ...texts rapt in fiery tongues.

REI, *n.*

Fig. 260: aside from a plant that is dying.

1. When you meet the owner of the municipal school, a woman with a thick waist, you nod, your salute to the bows this country bends on. A tick, you nod, and then she bows, so you nod again, unsure of what to do next. Her head has dropped nearly to her waist, but you're not going to do it. You don't know this thick waist from the prefecture.

REI, *n.*

Fig. 261: genki american sensei.

1. the girl at the counter shows her examples of the Hello Kitty prizes she could win for ¥1000.

RO, *n.*

Fig. 262: electronica and/or small appliances.

1. Fireplace; furnace. This has nothing to do with anything or any of it. They simply burned all of the submissions because they had a fireplace in the student apartment, and they could. This is ancillary. It predates the whole story. Everything else happens after.

2. the small window unit that operated both heat and cool in your room. roommate is generous and allows you to have it because she is showing you that she is strong. you accept. you sit in the doorway and tell her how it happened, the deafening wail that came from your mouth. you let the cold air fill the room.

ROKOTSU, *na.*

Fig. 263: a bathroom with an open ventilation system.

1. bare; uncovered. In the house of sliding doors, the bathroom has a cold aluminum door that opens onto the porch. Three slits in the wall above the toilet serve as the ventilation system as well as the mail drop. Lucky, if the mail drops into the toilet, she says the word Auspicious. She says, this one is written in invisible ink.

2. frank. you say to miyuki, you're taking advantage of me, and she asks you, (miyuki who promised greatness and funness) she asks you what it means. What do you mean.

3. let the machine get it.

4. a bare reel. a bare real. a bearish reality.

ROKUON, *n.*

Fig. 264: the rotating light of a cell phone display.

1. Sound recording;

1900 H.D. Scopine *Music and the Theatre: a Study of the Record of the Arts.* I. 17 the earliest sound recordings were kept for the purpose of archiving pieces of the oral tradition. Listen to the sound of the pear-shaped lute. Listen to the homonyms as they're plucked. **1934** B. Dover. 178 She kept the words that he had recorded onto her cellular telephonic device three days before he drowned. She played them. She played them. She played them. Save, forward, resave, he could still be sore from the gym. He says he's sore from going to the gym and where are you, I'm just calling to say that I like you and think that you are cute. There's a subtext, a post-test. If only you could play this message for your father, who doubts the existence of former happiness. If only for his mother, who scrapes your innards from the bone with a cake cutting and decorating spatula. **1982** F. Smoot, *Your Body, Your Self* 15 This isn't the first time someone has asked us, he said, and it's possible that he could have truly could have been sympathetic without PR reasons for being kind. You want to keep his voice. You want a copy to keep in a box in the back of your nightstand with the rest of your self-affirming post-its and with the piece of his old sweatshirt and with the papers you told his mother that you would "take care of" because she can't throw a damn thing away.

RON, *n.*

Fig. 265: a picture depicting conceptual "closed" and "openness."

1. Theory
2. His brother asked you to at least think about it, by which he meant, you don't want to remember this, you don't want to see what I think that I've done, I think I did this to him and I don't want to prove it to anyone, I don't want to look at the proof anymore.
3. He keeps theorizing: he was gone before long, before he hit the underwater ground, before anything bad could have happened. You believe it for a couple of years. You believe he could have had a head

wound that would have done everything. But you didn't see the evidence when you looked. You only saw a stitched up eyelid, the pallor of watery sleep.

RONIN, *n.*

Fig. 266: jean reno in costume.

1. Masterless samurai
2. you write on the pressed wooden prayer panels hung from nails
   on the trunk. *this is for your wish or dream.* she [mis]translates,
   for your prayers, for your last ditch
   attempt to say I am hurt and lost. they cannot read
   your romanji lettering, which means it's safe
   to say everything that will fit in three inches by five.

RONJIRU, *vb.*

Fig. 267: a stack of framed pictures taken from the wall.

1. argue
2. discuss. even in Japanese the euphemism sticks. let's discuss
   whether or not you should keep the watch you stole from the drawer,
   I thought it didn't work, when all it needed was to be wound. let's
   discuss whether or not you would have gotten married if you'd had
   the chance, let's see if you had any real impact. the dent you leave
   costs little.

ROTENBURO, *n.*

Fig. 268: a peep-show.

1. open-air bath

花見

HANAMI, *n.*

> *Fig. 1: cherry blossoms cascading toward the base of the falls.*

8. fanned out like a peacock's strut,
   the lanky limbs in full regalia. the dance of pink across the sky.

ワ

WA, *n.*

Fig. 269: a cedar chest full of underwear.

1. the names and places are lifted directly from your life: you weigh an orange in your hand
2. the clockwork of an island, the dials set to each temple along the 88 interval pilgrimage

WAKAJINI, *n.*

Fig. 270: amniotic fluid.

1. the gauge by which any euphemism for death is calculated as timely or un

WAKARU, *vb.*

Fig. 271: all your base are belong to us.

1. Meme looks over the top of the computer. She nods like a bridge to the thing you are explaining. *You stay me here*, she tells you in a letter slipped into your luggage, *I'm very luck.*
2. you wait for her quiet recognition to hold you again

WASABI, *n.*

Fig. 272: the trash on fire.

1. Japanese horseradish.

WATASHI, *pron.*

Fig. 273: the encyclopedia brittanica.

1. Watashi wa, watashi no, is never explained to your satisfaction. A trained and quiet line. a listening word.

ヲ

WO, *n.*

Fig. 274: a table of kana.

1. nothing starts with wo, other than wo, wo, unto the generations. it doesn't translate. most of this doesn't translate.

花見

HANAMI, *n.*

> *Fig. 1: cherry blossoms cascading toward the base of the falls.*

9. the shushing sound in your lungs

    rain washes your window with white translucent petals /the petals
    wash your window with their sodden bodies /the sodden body
    washes over your glassy face /the glass reflects the translucent petal
    of your face, holds a sodden body, washed like rain

N, *n.*

Fig. 275: a white board and markers.

1. the ending syllable (sound) of your name, of his name, of your names together. this is the one you practice the most. at American school the children show you the way. *nai, nai,* they draw an X over their chests to indicate that you've done it wrong, and they show you again on the white board, in the sand, with the chalk. *nai,* it's the girls, and they're being so nice about it, drawing it again, again.

花見

HANAMI, *n.*

Fig. 1: cherry blossoms cascading toward the base of the falls.

10. in the spring, the branches full to breaking
    scatter their heavy load upon these people who have stopped, laid
    themselves down under the white pink blanket
    and closed their eyes.

THANKS TO:

My husband, Karl, for his support; my mentors: Joyelle McSweeney for direction, and Kimberly Johnson for gifts of language and more than one kind of rice; Emily Fickenwirth for all the things; the early readers of my manuscript: Jessica M. English and Stephanie White; Akira Kusaka for his beautiful katakana; Eika Shinohara for her great care; the members of *April*: Steve N. Woodward, Aaron R. Allen, Mary L. Hedengren, and Sarah E. Jenkins; Amberlyn H. Kleinmen for giving me a translation dictionary; T.A. Noonan for this; and to Demaree and Harry Johnson for letting me in.

ACKNOWLEDGEMENTS:

Excerpts from Picture Dictionary appeared in *Lantern Review* and *Behind Closed Doors*.

BIOGRAPHY

Kristen Eliason holds an MFA in Creative Writing from the University of Notre Dame, where she was the recipient of the Sparks Prize. She is the author of a chapbook, *Yours,* and the co-founder of the online journal *Menagerie*. Her work appears in a variety of print and online journals, as well as two anthologies, The *Best of Kore Press*, and *Fire in the Pasture*. She lived in Japan in 2006, and currently lives in Northern California with her husband and their dog.

CPSIA information can be obtained at www.ICGtesting.com
Printed in the USA
LVOW02s1454160915

454250LV00003B/3/P